Further Ahead

Video Activity Book

Lynda Lawson

PUBLISHED BY THE PRESS SYNDICATE OF THE UNIVERSITY OF CAMBRIDGE
The Pitt Building, Trumpington Street, Cambridge CB2 1RP, United Kingdom

CAMBRIDGE UNIVERSITY PRESS
The Edinburgh Building, Cambridge CB2 2RU, United Kingdom
40 West 20th Street, New York, NY 10011–4211, USA
10 Stamford Road, Oakleigh, Melbourne 3166, Australia

Printed in the United Kingdom at the University Press, Cambridge

This Activity Book is an adaptation of the content of the Teacher's Guide.
ISBN 0 521 62645 5
ISBN 0 521 58779 4 Video and Teacher's Guide (VHS PAL)
ISBN 0 521 58778 6 Video and Teacher's Guide (VHS SECAM)
ISBN 0 521 58777 8 Video and Teacher's Guide (VHS NTSC)

Contents

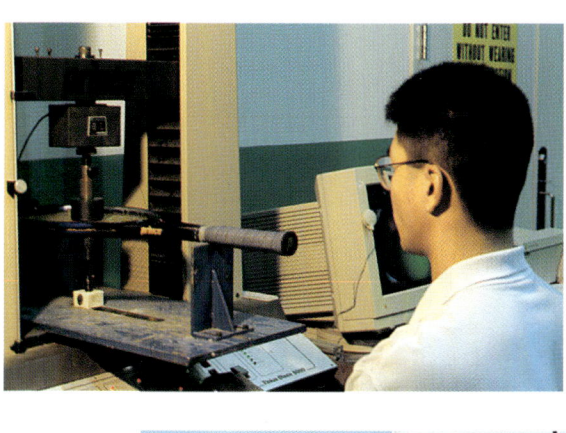

Introduction to the user

What is in the Video?

The Video contains four documentary sequences in which you see and hear real business people from around the world talking about and doing their work.

Sequence 1 Welcome to Prince (14 minutes)

In this sequence you visit the headquarters of the American sports goods company, Prince. You will see people:

- giving a presentation of their company
- dealing with customers and retailers
- talking about product development, design and testing
- describing their company culture

Sequence 2 The Delivery (12 minutes)

In this sequence you find out how Seafare, a British company specializing in shellfish, deals with a last-minute order. You will learn about:

- the business role of the company
- dealing with orders on the telephone
- quality control
- transportation problems

Sequence 3 What's in a brand name? (13 minutes)

You visit a British market research company, Leapfrog, as they work for Mars Chocolate. Mars is considering whether to change the brand name of a chocolate sold in the UK. You will see people:

- telephoning to make contact/arrangements
- having a briefing meeting
- presenting the history of their company
- doing market research and discussing the research findings

Sequence 4 The Solar Way (12 minutes)

In this sequence you visit BP Solar in Australia. You will see people:

- describing the production of solar cells
- presenting the market for this product
- demonstrating applications of this technology

The first part of this sequence is quite technical and will be useful if you need to understand or present technical processes in English.

How can the Video help improve my English?

Working with the Video and this Activity Book, you will:
- practise listening to authentic Business English
- build your Business English vocabulary
- consolidate your English grammar

The Activity Book is designed to help you work with the Video on your own, either at home or in a self-study centre. It prepares you for watching the Video, checks your understanding and gives you follow-up language practice. At the end of the book you will find answers to all the exercises and the videoscripts.
There are basically five stages in the Activity Book for each part you watch:

1 **Preview:** this can be a vocabulary check or short reading. It prepares you for watching the Video. Occasionally we suggest you watch the part of the Video without the sound.
2 **First view:** this gives you a general understanding of the part.
3 **Second view:** this gives you a more detailed understanding of the part. (Occasionally there is just one Viewing task for a part.)
4 **Language work, Further practice and Follow-up:** this is all follow-up work.
5 **Remembering key vocabulary:** this helps you record the important vocabulary.

Using the Answer key with videoscripts

Problems?
When you have done an exercise, look at the videoscript in the Answer key. What did you have a problem understanding? Was it vocabulary or pronunciation? Analysing this will help you understand better in the future.

New vocabulary
Choose a few useful expressions each time and make a note of them.

Revision
Next time you watch, take your vocabulary list, repeat the last part you saw and tick (✓) your words and expressions as you hear them.

Some suggestions for working on your own

1 All four sequences are divided into small parts. Start by working on just one or two parts at one time.
2 Don't try and understand every word you hear. Answer the questions in the book which are designed to help you understand the important information.
3 Don't forget to use the pictures to help you understand what people are saying.
4 Use the numbers on the screen to help you work with the Video.
5 Do regular revision sessions. Before you start a new part, look again at the last part you worked on.
6 Use a bilingual dictionary to help you translate words.

1 Welcome to Prince

Introduction

In this sequence you visit the American sports company, Prince.

You learn about the company's organization and culture, and see employees dealing with customers on the telephone, designing and testing products and meeting retail customers. You can use the sequence as a model for talking about your own company.

The sequence lasts 14 minutes and is organized like this:

Part 1 **An overview of the company**
    1.1 The products
    1.2 Location
    1.3 Ownership
Part 2 **Dealing with the public**
Part 3 **Product innovation**
Part 4 **Tele-sales to retailers**
Part 5 **Design and testing**
Part 6 **A retail customer comes to visit**
Part 7 **Company culture**
    7.1 The dress code
    7.2 The working atmosphere

Part 1 An overview of the company (00:00)

Introduction (00:00)

Watch from the beginning to 00:48 to get a general idea of the company and its products. Then make questions using these prompts.

1 What / Prince / make?
2 Where / headquarters?
3 Where / products / made? 🔑

What do you think the answers will be?

1.1 The products (00:49)

Preview

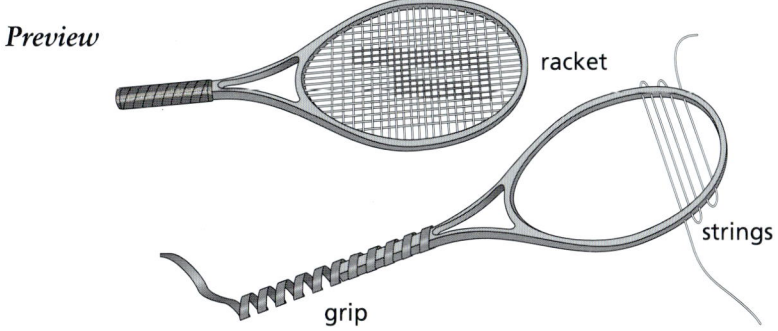

racket

strings

grip

Read the conversation on the right and answer the question.

What do you think *accessory* means here? Check its meaning in your dictionary.

> Do you sell grips and strings for tennis rackets?

> Yes, they're upstairs in the accessories section.

Viewing task

Charlie Peifer, President and Chief Executive Officer of Prince, talks about their range of products. Correct these statements.

1 Prince is a small racket company.
2 Prince makes tennis, badminton and squash rackets and accessories.
3 Most of their racket manufacturing is done in mainland China.

Further practice

Read this advertisement and then write a paragraph about this company, using expressions such as
*We make ... , We also sell ... ,
Most of our manufacturing is done ... .*

Alternatively, write about a company you know.

OFFICE MAKER
Specialists in office furniture

Desks, chairs, computer workstations, filing cabinets, desk lamps and deskside bins.

All designed in Australia. Made in Indonesia from top-quality materials.

1.2 Location (01:26)

Preview

Match the words and phrases on the left with the definitions on the right.

1 throughout   A spread all over an area
2 to coordinate   B in all parts of
3 distributor   C to organize / to make people or things work together
4 scattered   D a person or company that supplies goods to businesses
                      or shops that sell them

First view

Listen to Charlie Peifer and decide which map is correct.

Location of Prince Headquarters

Second view

Watch again. Where else does Prince have offices?

Further practice

Write a paragraph describing the location of your office or school in relation to the capital city of your country. Use some of these expressions, if possible:
We're headquartered in ... , which is ... . We also have ... .

8

1.3 Ownership (02:00)

Preview

Check the meaning of these words and phrases in your dictionary.

to acquire   to connect
to be comprised of   responsible for
column

Now use the words and phrases in these sentences. You will need to use one of them twice. Use the correct forms of the verbs.

1 Who is .... the design of the squash rackets?
2 This year my department .... about 40 people who work in four different groups.
3 Last year our company .... a smaller company in Italy.
4 A new road now .... our headquarters to the city.
5 In the middle of the square is a .... with a statue on it.
6 We plan to .... some land north of the airport for our new headquarters.

Viewing task

**Charlie Peifer talks about who owns Prince.
Complete the diagram.**

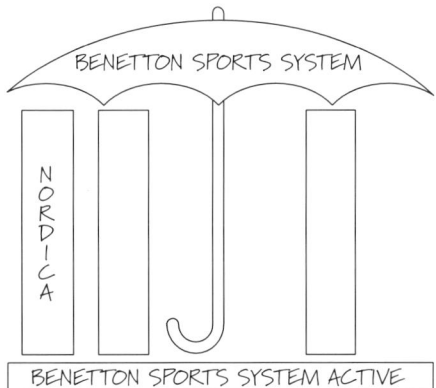

Language work

Notice how the passive form of the verb is used to describe what happens to someone or something:

In 1989 we were acquired by the Benetton Sports System.

Rewrite these sentences in the passive. For example:

Professional tennis players buy our rackets.
Our rackets are bought by professional tennis players.

1 Tennis players design all our goods.
2 Our office in Singapore coordinates our work in Asia.
3 An American company designed our headquarters.
4 The director organized today's meeting.

Further practice

Write a description of the ownership of Prince using the diagram above and the following words and phrases: *comprised of, columns, to deal with, connected by, responsible for.*

Alternatively, write about the structure and ownership of a company you know. Use as many of the words and phrases above as possible.

Remembering key vocabulary

When you have corrected your work and looked at the videoscript for Part 1, note about five words or expressions that are important to you in the space provided.

nouns	verbs	expressions

Revise these words and expressions later by watching this part again and ✓ ticking the words and expressions as you hear them. Try to remember them in their context.

Part 2   Dealing with the public (02:52)

Preview

In the address on the right, the number 08638 is the "zip". What do you think this is in American English? Check its meaning in your dictionary.

Mr Jerome Allgood
226 Dryden Avenue
Trenton, NJ 08638

First view

Dawn Smith, who works in Customer Services, talks to a customer on the phone and about her work. Watch the first half where she is on the phone. What makes you think she is good at her job?

Second view

Now watch the second half where Dawn talks about her job. Answer these questions.

1 What does she say she likes about her job?
2 What are her three responsibilities?
   – educating consumers about .... our products.
   – telling them about the .... that we sell.
   – handling warranty ....

Language work

Watch Dawn again and complete the sentences below.

Then match these stages of the conversation with the sentences. Two of the sentences are in the same stage.

establishing a need   getting key information   confirming
closing the conversation

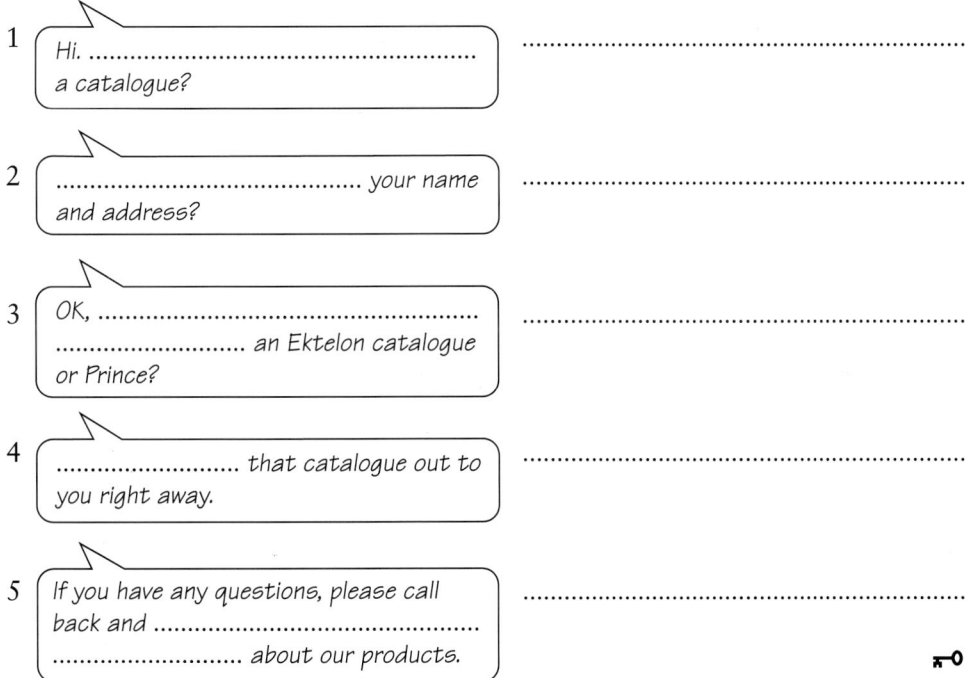

1 Hi. ....
   a catalogue?   ....

2 .... your name   ....
   and address?

3 OK, ...
   .... an Ektelon catalogue
   or Prince?

4 .... that catalogue out to   ....
   you right away.

5 If you have any questions, please call   ....
   back and ....
   .... about our products.

Further practice

Read the videoscript on page 57. Write what you think the caller is saying.

Part 3 Product innovation (04:02)

Preview

Check the meaning of these words in your dictionary.

size
to innovate
dimensional
length

body — head

cross-section

First view

Dave Holland, who is a marketing director
at Prince, talks about the changes in tennis
racket design over the years. There have
been three major dimensional changes.
Put them in the order they happened.

long body rackets ☐
oversized heads on rackets ☐
wide body rackets ☐ 🔑

1971–1975
HOWARD HEAD—inventor
Frustrated with his tennis game, Howard Head
is introduced to the Prince Ball Machine. Soon
he feels compelled to work out a few design
bugs in the Ball Machine. Before you know
it, he is majority owner and Chairman of the
Board. The Ball Machine prospers but Head
still struggles with off center hits and lack
of control, motivating him to invent the first
patented Prince oversized racquet as we
know it today.

Second view

Listen again to Dave Holland.
Are these statements true or false?

1 Before 1976 most players were
   playing with wooden rackets.
2 Howard Head designed the
   oversized-head racket in the eighties.
3 Wide body rackets produce more power.
4 The long body racket gives you four benefits.
5 The long body is the last possible dimensional change. 🔑

Language work

Complete the sentences from the videoscript with the correct form of the verb in brackets.

Tennis equipment [1] .... *(change)* considerably in the last 20 years. If we go back to before 1976, really most players [2] .... *(play)* with wooden rackets. And you notice the wood rackets' very small head sizes. Howard Head [3] .... *(come)* along and not only innovated the ski industry with the first metal ski but innovated the tennis industry with the first dimensional change in tennis rackets. And that essentially means he invented the oversized head and, if you compare that to a wooden racket, you can see quite clearly you've got a much larger head in the oversize racket. That [4] .... *(happen)* in the mid-seventies.

Then the next major innovation occurred with another dimensional change in the rackets which [5] .... *(be)* the wide body, and wide bodies allowed for greater stiffness in rackets, therefore producing much more power.

And today the next biggest innovation is also dimensional and that is length. Here is our new Mach 1000. The Prince Long Body racket [6] .... *(give)* you five major benefits. They are more power, more control, more spin, more reach and more comfort.

Further practice

Write a short history of the changes in this product, paying special attention to the form of the verb. Use the information given here and on the next page.

The 300 model desk telephone (1937)
– *bell included in the telephone for the first time*

The coloured telephone (1954)
– *popular with those who wanted the telephone to match their furniture*

The "trimphone" (1968)
– *major dimensional changes*
– *push buttons replaced dial in 1976*

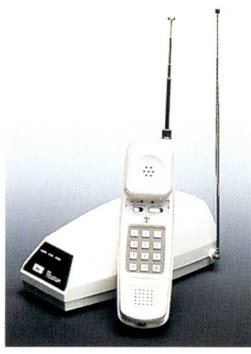

The cordless phone and the mobile phone (1980s)
– gave freedom of movement
– mobile phones could be used in cars

The mobile phone in the 1990s (Here the Motorola StarTAC™)
– battery lasts up to 50 hours
– weight: 110g
– size: 98 by 57 by 23 mm
– caller line identity (you can see who is calling)
– data capable (with a data card you can go online: receive information from a PC, surf the Internet)

Alternatively, write about developments in a product you are familiar with.

Remembering key vocabulary

When you have corrected your work and looked at the videoscripts for Parts 2 and 3, note words and expressions that are important to you in the space provided.

nouns	verbs	adjectives	expressions

Revise these words and expressions later by watching these parts again and ✓ ticking the words and expressions as you hear them. Try to remember them in their context.

Part 4 Tele-sales to retailers (06:17)

Preview

The following phrases occur in the videoscript. Choose the phrases which are closest in meaning to them.

1 I'm running a special on ...
   A I'm selling a product at an unusually low price
   B I'm selling a product at its normal price
   C I'm selling a product for runners

2 I wanted to let you know ...
   A I wanted to introduce you to someone ...
   B I wanted to persuade you ...
   C I wanted to tell you ...   🔑

First view

Mary McDermott in tele-sales
talks to Tony Pratolini, a sports
equipment retailer. Take down his
order on the form.

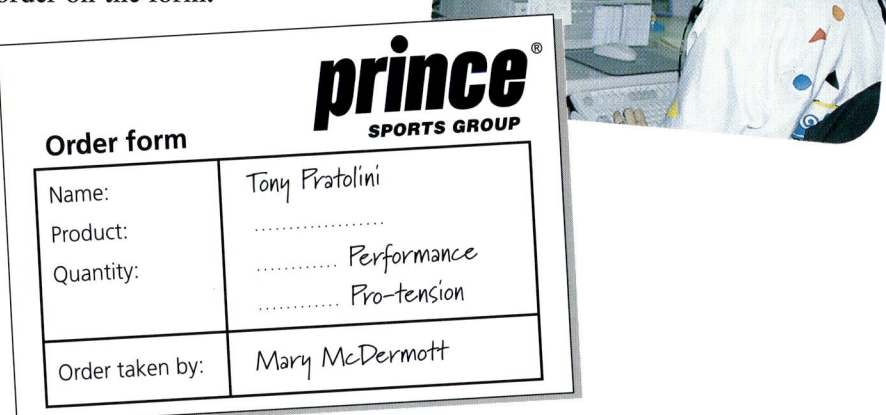

Order form	
Name:	Tony Pratolini
Product:	....
Quantity:	.... Performance
	.... Pro-tension
Order taken by:	Mary McDermott

🔑

Second view

Watch again. Who said the following sentences: Mary or Tony?

1 (Fine. And yourself?)

2 (Listen, the reason I'm calling you today is to make sure, one, you received the catalogue ...)

3 (What are the prices on the different colours?)

4 (That's a pretty good deal.)

5 (OK, I'll give you a call in a couple of weeks to check in again.)

6 (Take care.)   🔑

Language work

Listen and read the videoscript on page 59. Notice how the conversation consists
of different stages: (1) polite conversation, (2) business, and (3) finishing the call.
Underline the sentences or phrases which show the start of each stage.   🔑

Part 5 Design and testing (08:07)

Preview

Watch to 08:49 without the sound. Which feature(s) of the tennis racket is Susan Mac talking about, do you think? Choose from this list:

length   weight   comfort   colour   power

First view

Listen to Brian Blonski, a research and development director, talk about computer-aided design. Choose the correct answer to this question.

In what way does computer-aided design help?

A It cuts manufacturing costs.
B It makes the racket look attractive.
C It makes sure all the pieces of the racket fit together.

Second view

According to Brian Blonski, what can the tests predict? Choose the correct answer.

A The product's performance.
B How long the product will last.
C Under what conditions it will break.

Further practice

Watch from 08:07 to 08:49 again. Susan is talking to Vicky at their factory in China. Complete the notes Vicky made during the call.

Call from Sue
Problem with ....
She needs another .... sent out by ....
She will fax ....

Remembering key vocabulary

When you have corrected your work and looked at the videoscripts for Parts 4 and 5, note words and expressions that are important to you in the space provided.

expressions for the telephone	nouns	verbs	adjectives

Revise these words and expressions later by watching these parts again and ✓ ticking the words and expressions as you hear them. Try to remember them in their context.

Part 6 A retail customer comes to visit (09:56)

Preview

line = product line = range of products

Watch the conversation without the sound. What words or expressions do you expect to hear?

Viewing task

Jeannette Samuels, a retailer, comes to see Bob Fenton, a national accounts director. Watch and answer these questions.

1 What time is her appointment?
2 Does she know Bob Fenton already? How do you know this?
3 Has she been to the Prince headquarters before? If so, when?
4 What are they going to talk about?
5 What tells you Bob may have been promoted recently?

Language work

Look at the videoscript on pages 60–1 and find:
1 a way of suggesting something
2 a way of agreeing to someone's suggestion
3 a way of offering politely to do something
4 three ways of welcoming someone

Now complete these short conversations with the phrases you have found.
5 A:.. get you a drink. What would you like?
   B: A glass of orange juice, please.
6 A:.. have lunch tomorrow?
   B: ....
7 A:..
   B: Thanks. It's good to see you too.

Learning strategy

In social situations it is often difficult to reply quickly and appropriately in a second language. Make a list of typical expressions used in social situations and an appropriate reply. Test yourself by covering up the reply.

7.1 The dress code (11.50)

Preview

How would you describe the dress code in your company or in a company you would like to work for? Choose words from this list.

relaxed   stiff   formal   informal   casual   comfortable   smart   tidy

Viewing task

Listen to Charlie Peifer again and to Rick Margin, a Marketing Vice-President. They both talk about the dress code. Correct these sentences.

1 According to Charlie Peifer, the business culture in the US – and around the world – is changing very slowly.
2 According to Charlie Peifer, smart clothes make people work better.
3 Rick Margin says you can wear any sports clothes at Prince.
4 Rick Margin says people who come to Prince are shocked by the dress code.
5 The casual dress code is the reason Rick works there.

Language work

Notice that *have to* is used to express obligation imposed from outside (for example, an obligation imposed by a company/work situation).

There was a time when people had to wear white shirts ...
The policy actually is you have to wear Benetton ...

Read the chart and write sentences about Tom Mullen's past and present obligations.

		Obligations
1988	Tom started work on the factory floor of a South Korean company in Britain.	to wear protective clothing to start at 7.00 a.m.
Today	Tom is a manager in the same factory.	to wear a suit and tie to visit South Korea regularly

Alternatively, write about the obligations associated with your job now and in the past.

7.2 The working atmosphere (12:37)

Preview

Check the meaning of these words in your dictionary. Then use them to complete the sentences below.

intimate   youthful   fun   enjoyable

1 This year's conference was much more .... than last year's.
2 Although he was in his sixties, he behaved in a very .... way.
3 The small restaurant had a really .... atmosphere and was a favourite for a romantic dinner.
4 She is such a .... person that everyone likes inviting her to parties.

Viewing task

Brian Blonski and Rick Margin talk about working at Prince. Watch and answer these questions.

1 What does Brian Blonski say is a "very positive thing"?
2 What was a problem for him in his previous job?
3 What does Prince's smaller size make it easier for him to do?
4 What is surprising about what Rick Margin says about his tennis playing?
5 According to Rick Margin, what brings people together?
6 What does Brian Blonski like best about his job?

Remembering key vocabulary

When you have corrected your work and looked at the videoscripts for Parts 6 and 7, note words or expressions that are important to you in the space provided.

nouns	verbs	expressions

Revise these words and expressions later by watching these parts again and ✓ ticking the words and expressions as you hear them. Try to remember them in their context.

2 The Delivery

Introduction

In this sequence you see how Seafare, a British company, deals with a last-minute order for shellfish from a French supermarket. You will learn some language for dealing with orders and making arrangements on the telephone, as well as language related to transportation and quality control.

Read this information about Seafare and answer the questions.

Fact file: Seafare

Business: buying and selling shellfish, especially mussels and oysters

Main customers: French supermarket chains

Main suppliers: fishermen in the UK, the Republic of Ireland and Holland

Headquarters: at Kingsbridge, Devon in the UK

Number of staff: six people in Devon. As well as the offices in Devon, Seafare has a share in a shellfish purification plant outside Boulogne in France.

Ownership: Chris Phippen and Caroline Poultney

Turnover: £1.5 million

History: started in 1988 by Chris Phippen and Caroline Poultney

---

What are the major concerns for a company like this, do you think? Choose some from this list or think of others.

product development	company image
speed of delivery	freshness of their product
quality of their product	reliability of service
health and safety	constant changes in technology

The sequence lasts 12 minutes and is organized like this:

Part 1   The order (00:00)

Preview

Check the meaning of these nouns and verbs in your dictionary. Then use them in the sentences below. Use the correct forms of the verbs.

promotion   to include
top-up   to pick something up
to deliver

1 They have received our order and they will .... it tomorrow.
2 Is it too late for me to ask for a .... to yesterday's order?
3 The price .... a charge for service.
4 We plan to give free samples to the supermarkets as a ....
5 The lorries now .... the fish from the factory every morning. ⚿

Kroonton: the name of a packaging company
de Koeijer: the name of a transportation company

First view

Chris   Caroline   Rebecca

Frederic, from the French supermarket company, Auchan, calls Caroline at home with a last-minute order for mussels. Caroline then goes into the office to discuss the order with Chris and to get Rebecca to deal with it. Answer these questions with short answers.

1 What quantity of mussels does Frederic want to order?
2 Is Caroline sure they can supply the order?
3 When does Frederic want the order delivered?
4 Is this a promotional order or just a top-up?
5 Who does Chris ask Rebecca to contact?   ⚿

Second view

Watch the part where Caroline is on the phone (00:15–00:43) and guess what Frederic might be saying. 🔑

Language work

Look at these words from the videoscript. Mark the main stressed syllables in each. For example:

a <u>top</u>-up

1 actually
2 within
3 promotion
4 ordinary
5 delivery

Now mark the main words stressed in these short sentences.

6 I'm not actually in the office yet.
7 I'll call you back.
8 Well, it's a bit late.

Then watch this part again and check your answers. 🔑

Part 2 About Seafare (01:59)

Preview

Check the meaning and the pronunciation of the following verbs in your dictionary.

to base   to look for
to supply   to source (a product)
to liaise   to evolve something

First view

Caroline and Chris talk about Seafare's work. Which diagram best describes what Caroline says? 🔑

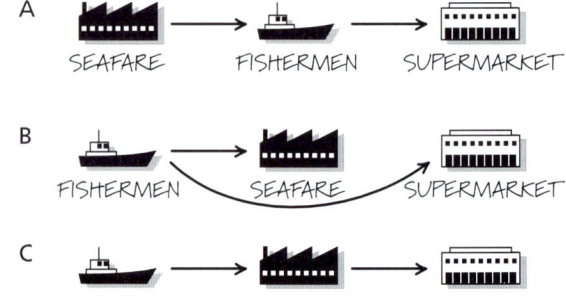

Second view

Listen to Chris and answer these questions.

1 Where does he say they buy mussels?
2 Where does he say they sell mussels?   ⌐O

Language work

Read the fact file below and write a paragraph about Sun Fruit, using these verbs:

evolve   liaise   look for   source   supply

Fact file: Sun Fruit

Business: buying and selling tropical fruit, especially bananas and mangoes

Main customers: supermarket chains in France, Britain and Holland

Main suppliers: growers in Africa and India

Main strength: fast and efficient transportation

Now write a paragraph about a company you know which has a similar kind of business.   ⌐O

Remembering key vocabulary

When you have corrected your work and looked at the videoscripts for Parts 1 and 2, note words and expressions that are important to you in the space provided.

nouns	verbs	other words	expressions

Revise these words and expressions later by watching these parts again and ✓ ticking the words and expressions as you hear them. Try to remember them in their context.

Part 3 Dealing with the order (03:38)

Preview

Read the following sentences and answer the question.

> Goods are delivered to the supermarket every night. They come from the company *platform* for the area. All the supermarkets in our area are served by the same *platform*.

What do you think *platform* means in this context?   ⚷

Viewing task

Rebecca at Seafare calls Jap at Kroonton in Holland about the order. Watch this part and then complete the fax from Rebecca confirming this last-minute order.

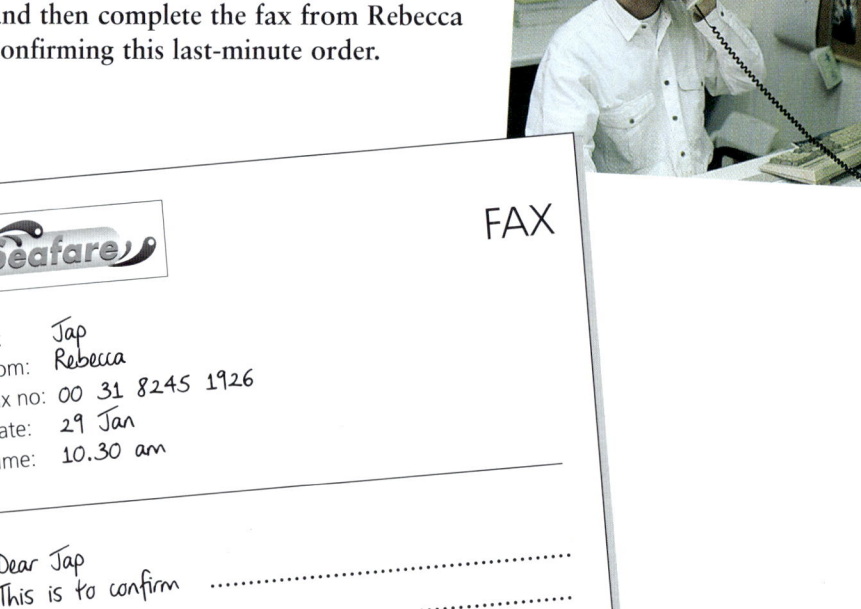

Seafare   FAX

To: Jap
From: Rebecca
Fax no: 00 31 8245 1926
Date: 29 Jan
Time: 10.30 am
_____

Dear Jap
This is to confirm ....

....

....
Thanks very much ....

....

....

Best wishes
         Rebecca

⚷

Language work

Watch again and complete the sentences with the correct expressions.

> 1 .... Rebecca
> 2 ....

> Good, good. Um, I'm 3 ....
> .... we've just had a
> last-minute addition to the orders for
> Auchan.

> 4 .... I'll, I'll 5 ....
> ....
> .... to confirm
> that then.

A

Part 4 Sourcing and Quality (04:34)

4.1 Dutch mussels (05:05)

Preview

The words and phrases below describe some of Seafare's preparation of mussels. Check their meaning in your dictionary.

B

	Process	Picture
selection	☐	☐
landing	☐	☐
packing	☐	☐
collection from seabed	☐	☐
moving by conveyor belt	☐	☐

C

Watch up to 05:42 without the sound and number these processes as you see them.
Then match pictures A–E with the processes. ⚷

Viewing task

Chris talks about how Dutch mussels are sorted. Answer these three questions.

D

1 How are the mussels divided?
2 Which kind of mussels are for the French market?
3 How many tons of mussels will Seafare move this year? ⚷

E

4.2 Purification and Grading (05:44)

Preview

Check the meaning and pronunciation of these words in your dictionary.

purify   purification   classify   classification

First view

You are going to see Chris at Seafare's purification station at Wimereux, near Boulogne. Watch him up to 06:35. Then draw a simple diagram, using these words, to describe what he says.

– mussels from Ireland, other parts of France, Wales, Scotland
– purification plant in Wimereux
– Boulogne transport depot
– rest of France

Second view

Listen from 06:36. Complete these sentences about mussel grading classifications.

Grade A classification: You can eat the mussels ....
Grade B classification: The mussels need to ....
Grade C classification: The mussels need twice ....
....

Part 5 Arranging transportation (07:23)

Viewing task

Rebecca calls Eric at de Koeijer's and then speaks to Caroline in the Seafare office. Answer these questions.

1 What do Rebecca and Eric talk about first?
2 What does she want to find out from Eric?
3 What does Rebecca promise Eric that she will do?

4 What does Rebecca do after the phone call?
5 What does Caroline ask Rebecca to do?
6 Why do you think Caroline asks Rebecca to do this?   🔑

Language work

Notice these two ways of talking about the future:

1 So de Koeijer is loading at three o'clock or so.
2 I'll send you a fax.

Which one talks about future actions that have already been planned?
Which one talks about future actions that have *not* already been planned?

Complete these sentences with the verb in brackets. Use the verb either in the present continuous tense or with *will*.

1 Caroline's not here at the moment, but I .... (leave) a note
   for her.
2 We .... (go) to Seoul next Monday.
3 I'm afraid he can't come next Friday. He .... (spend) the day
   in Hong Kong.
4 I'm busy this morning, but I .... (phone) you this afternoon.
5 Thanks for your fax. We .... (discuss) your suggestions this
   afternoon and we .... (call) you tomorrow.   🔑

Remembering key vocabulary

When you have corrected your work and looked at the videoscripts for Parts
3–5, note words and expressions that are important to you in the space
provided.

nouns	verbs	other words	expressions

Revise these words and expressions later by watching these parts again and ✓
ticking the words and expressions as you hear them. Try to remember them in
their context.

6.1 Choosing the route (08:40)

Preview

Check the meaning of the following words and expressions in your dictionary.

ferry   rush hour
to cut the corner   to hold someone up
to bear in mind   cross-country

Match the two halves of the sentences.

1 We went cross-country   A you'll save hours of driving.
2 If you cut the corner here   B you'll miss the last ferry.
3 I left early   C to avoid the main roads.
4 It's important to bear in mind D when the weather's bad.
5 If the traffic holds you up   E to avoid the rush hour.
6 The ferry can be very slow   F the possible problems with transport. ⚷

Viewing task

Caroline has a choice of two
routes for delivering the mussels
from Yerseke in Holland to Lièvin
in France. Which does she choose,
A or B?

Route A

Route B

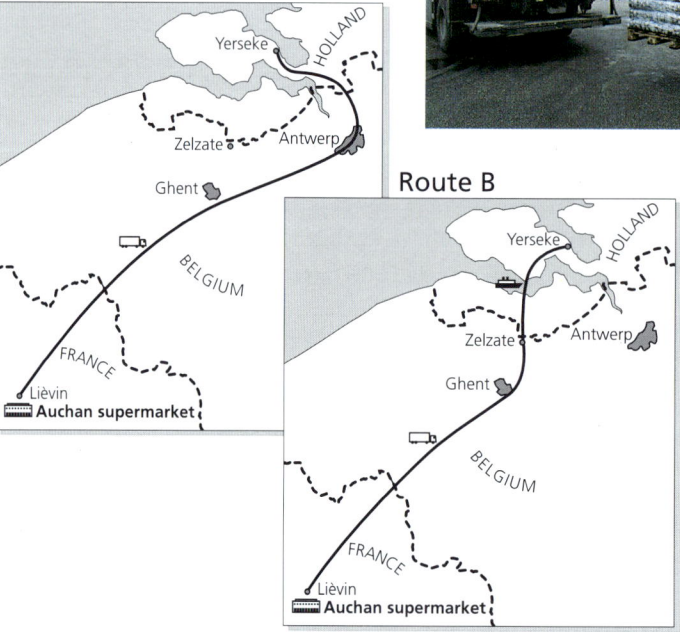

⚷

Language work

Caroline talks about possible future actions by saying: "We could either go by road or we could take the ferry." Make sentences about similar actions from these prompts. For example:

you / use this supplier / try another one
You could either use this supplier or (you could) try another one.

1 they / increase the price / reduce the quantity in each bag
2 I / write a letter / send a fax
3 we / deliver directly to the shops / pay for distribution
4 he / meet you on Wednesday / phone you this afternoon
5 we / get a taxi / wait for a bus

Then write about five sentences using *I could either ... or ...*, to describe your plans for tomorrow, the weekend, next week, your next holiday and next year.　🔑

6.2 Transportation problems (09:25)

Preview

Make a list of the transportation problems Seafare might face.

Viewing task

Caroline talks about the things that can go wrong. Does she mention any of the problems you thought of?
Watch and complete the notes.
1 Man-made problems: .... and ....
   ....
2 .... problems: for example, ...　🔑

6.3 Delivery to the supermarkets (09:48)

Preview

Read the following sentence and answer the question.

> We have a number of *depots* throughout the country, so your order will be delivered from the *depot* which is nearest to you.

What do you think *depot* means? Check the answer in your dictionary.

Viewing task

Chris and Caroline summarize Seafare's
work. Are these statements true?
Correct them if they are not.

1 Seafare always delivers directly to
   the supermarket.
2 Seafare's role has changed over the years.
3 Seafare has to respond very quickly to
   orders.
4 Some of the time Seafare delivers on time.

Language work

Find words or phrases in the videoscript which mean the same as these
definitions.

1 someone who does business for someone else ....
2 the place where you are going ....
3 a machine that carries people or things ....
4 to be pleased because you can do a particular thing ....
5 belonging to a particular area ....
6 items for sale ....
7 a request for something to be supplied to you ....

Further practice

Write a description of Seafare as a company, using the fact file on page 20 and
including any information from the sequence.

Remembering key vocabulary

When you have corrected your work and looked at the videoscript for Part 6,
note words and expressions that are important to you in the space provided.

nouns	verbs	other words	expressions

Revise these words and expressions later by watching this part again and ✓
ticking the words and expressions as you hear them. Try to remember them in
their context.

3 What's in a brand name?

Introduction

In this sequence, we see Mars Chocolate commission some market research into a possible new name for a chocolate bar. We watch the market research company at work and see how they present their findings to Mars Chocolate.

Thinking point: Do you know of a product which has been renamed? Do you know why this was done, and what was the impact of the change?

The sequence lasts 13 minutes and is organized like this:

Part 1 **Making contact**
Part 2 **Visiting Leapfrog**
Part 3 **How Leapfrog started**
Part 4 **The group discussions**
    4.1 Organizing the groups
    4.2 Qualitative market research
    4.3 A group discussion
Part 5 **The research findings**

Part 1 Making contact (00:00)

Preview

Check the meaning of these words in your dictionary. Then use them in the sentences below.

consumer	loyalist
brand	to brief
to assess	project

1 I need to .... you on the new products we've introduced.
2 These questions are designed to .... your satisfaction with our service.
3 This .... of sports clothes is very popular with young people.
4 It has taken us two months to complete this ....
5 Many .... choose our products because of their good quality.
6 It can be difficult to persuade brand .... to buy a new kind of soap or washing powder.

First view

Chris Hardy of Mars Chocolate calls
Andrea Berlowitz of Leapfrog, a
qualitative market research company.
He wants to commission some market
research about a possible brand name
change.

Watch this part and answer this question.

Are Mars considering:

A changing the name of the chocolate bar Galaxy to Dove in the UK?
B changing the name of the chocolate bar Dove to Galaxy in the UK?   🔑

Second view

Watch again. Are these statements true or false? Give reasons for your answers.

	True	False
1 Chris and Andrea don't know each other.	☐	☐
2 Chris wants to find out what people think of the change in name.	☐	☐
3 Chris wants to find out the opinions only of Galaxy eaters.	☐	☐
4 Chris and Andrea are going to meet soon to discuss the project.	☐	☐
5 Andrea is going to work alone on this project.	☐	☐
6 Chris wants the results of the market research within eight weeks.	☐	☐ 🔑

Language work

Watch again from 00:41 and complete these sentences used to signal "let's talk about business".

Andrea

> Very well, very well.
> 1 .... ?

Chris

> Andrea, we're looking to commission
> some consumer research and
> 2 ....
> ....

Watch again and complete the sentences they use to find a time to meet.

Andrea

> Well, I suppose what we ought to do is have a brief, a briefing meeting some time, shouldn't we?

Chris

> Er, let me just have a look. I think towards the end of this week would be great if that's OK for you.
> 3 ....
> Friday?

Andrea

> Friday. Yeah, 4 ....
> ....

Andrea

> 5 ....
> just before lunch?

In some forms of English (e.g. British and Australian) it is not polite to ask for or suggest things in a very direct, definite way. For example, instead of saying "We must have a briefing meeting this week" Andrea says "*I suppose* what we ought to do is have a briefing meeting *some time, shouldn't we?*" The phrases in italic are those she uses to make her suggestion sound like a possibility, not a certainty.

Find other examples in the sentences above of phrases that express possibility.

Which modal verb is used here to express possibility, rather than certainty? ⚿

Part 2 Visiting Leapfrog (02:17)

Preview

Complete the definitions below with these words and phrases. Check your
answers in the dictionary.

recipe   disrupt
sample   in detail
regular

1 If you study something .... , you do it very carefully, looking at all
   the minor points.
2 A .... of people is a group of people selected to provide information
   about a larger group.
3 If you .... something, you stop it from continuing as planned.
4 A .... is a list of ingredients, with instructions on how to cook them.
5 A .... reader of a magazine is someone who often reads it.   ⚲

First view

Listen to Chris Hardy tell Andrea Berlowitz and
Sue about the research he wants Leapfrog to do.
Answer this question.

What *two new* things are discussed in the meeting
which Chris did not mention to Andrea in their
phone conversation?   ⚲

Second view

Listen to the conversation again and identify the words or phrases which mean
the same as these words or phrases.

1 hello   ....   5 limited number
2 (to) start   ....   6 good   ....
3 aims   ....   7 (to) finish   ....
4 exactly the same ....   ⚲

Language work

Look at the videoscript on page 69 and complete the chart with examples from
the videoscript.

form	used to talk about	examples
will + infinitive	a spontaneous offer	
will + *be* + *ing* form (future progressive)	an action which is expected to happen as a matter of course	

⚲

Complete these sentences with either *will* + infinitive or *will* + *be* + *ing*, using the verbs in brackets.

1 They .... (move) offices some time next year because they need to be nearer Tokyo.
2 "Are you coming to lunch?"
"Yes, I .... (come) in a minute. I just have to send this fax first."
3 "Could you check you have received our order?"
"Sure. I .... (look) on the computer now."
4 We don't need to call her now as we .... (see) her at tomorrow's meeting anyway.
5 "Can you send me that report today, please?"
"Of course. We .... (fax) it through to you this afternoon."

Further practice

Watch again from 02:43 and complete these sentences used to introduce a colleague.

Andrea

> Um, 1 .... Sue over.
> I 2 .... meet her.
> She's going to be working on the project. Sue,
> 3 .... over?

Watch again from 03:00 and complete the phrases where Chris refers to his earlier conversation with Andrea.

Chris

> OK, well really, 4 ....
> .... , Andrea ...

Chris

> Right, well, 5 .... ,
> Andrea and I 6 ....
> .... , I think
> we're probably ...

Watch again from 03:57 and note how Andrea concludes the meeting and suggests lunch.

Andrea

> Great. 7 ....
> .... , doesn't it? 8 ....
> .... some lunch ...

Remembering key vocabulary

When you have corrected your work and looked at the videoscripts for Parts 1 and 2, note words and expressions that are important to you in the space provided.

nouns	verbs	other words	expressions for meetings

Revise these words and expressions later by watching these parts again and ✓ ticking the words and expressions as you hear them. Try to remember them in their context.

Part 3   How Leapfrog started (04:12)

Preview

Check the meaning of these words and phrases in your dictionary.

to set up   prior to
premises   to advertise

Windsor: the town near London where Leapfrog is located

Viewing task

The two original directors of Leapfrog, Andrea Berlowitz and Judy Taylor, talk about Leapfrog's beginnings. Answer these questions.

1 Is Leapfrog a young or an old company?
2 What tells you the company wasn't very big at the beginning?
3 What tells you the company is successful?
4 How did Judy and Andrea meet each other?
5 What is Andrea's work background?
6 Why did they start Leapfrog?   ⚷

Part 4 The group discussions (05:25)

4.1 Organizing the groups (05:33)

Preview

Read this advertisement and answer the question.

What does *to recruit* mean, do you think?

Check in your dictionary, if you are not sure.

Northern Recruitment Agency

Do you find it hard to find the right employees? Let us help! With over 25 years of recruiting experience, we can help find the right person for that essential job.

Viewing task

Sue calls Eunice, who recruits groups to be interviewed. Complete the note Eunice made for herself.

> Sue from Leapfrog
> .... groups of ....
> .... o'clock on Tuesday .... March.
> At .... for .... to ....

Language work

Notice how Sue asks Eunice for help: "I was just wondering, would you be able to help us with recruiting ... ." This is another example of making a request polite by using language of possibility rather than certainty.

What could you say in these situations? Make polite requests with the verb *wonder*. For example:

You want someone to fax you today.
I was wondering if you could fax me today.

1 You need your colleague's help with a report you are writing.
2 You need to ask your supervisor for permission to leave work early today.
3 You want to find somewhere to stay in your colleague's home town.
4 You need some information from the marketing department about a new product.

4.2 Qualitative market research (06:03)

Preview

Qualitative research is concerned with quality rather than quantity. In research terms this usually means interviews in which people give their opinions, which are later analysed.

Quantitative research, on the other hand, is concerned with large samples that will produce statistically significant results.

Check the meaning of the following words and phrases in your dictionary.

to expose   to gain   in depth

Viewing task

Listen and complete these sentences with one word.

1 The group discussions are very
....
2 There are between .... and
.... people in a group.
3 People talk quite .... and in
.... about the topic in hand.
4 You expose them to products or
packaging and gain their ....
5 The discussions are very
....

4.3 A group discussion (06:45)

Preview

Check the meaning of the following words in your dictionary. Then use them in the sentences below.

smooth   indulgent   packaging   shelf

1 The .... is very colourful in order to appeal to young people.
2 My grandparents were very .... and gave me a lot of presents when I was a child.
3 Could you pass me the blue file on the .... behind you, please?
4 It's hard to drive on this road because the surface is not ....

The name (06:47)

Before you watch the first part of the discussion in which the group discusses their associations with the word *dove*, write the words you associate with it in the word spider.

dove

What kind of chocolate bar would you expect Dove to be?

Viewing task

Watch the discussion. See if the group has the same ideas as you about words they associate with *dove* and the same expectations about the kind of chocolate Dove would be.

The situation (07:42)

You have just heard the group say Dove is a bar for a "very relaxed" and "very indulgent" moment. When would you eat this chocolate?

at work   in the evening   for lunch   as a snack   in a group   alone

Viewing task

The group talks more about when they would eat the chocolate. When would you expect them to eat Dove? Watch and see if you are right.

The packaging (08:33)

Viewing task

Watch this part and answer this question.

Overall, is the group positive or negative about the packaging? ⚷

Changing the name (10:02)

Viewing task

Watch this part and answer this question.

Overall, is the group positive or negative about the possible name change? ⚷

Language work

Here are some of the ways the discussion group described the packaging. Decide whether each phrase has a positive or negative meaning. Write P or N next to it.

1 it works very well ....
2 it stands out ....
3 it portrays the right image ....
4 Just like anything else on the shelf really. ....
5 the writing is too hard, it's too straight .... ⚷

Part 5 The research findings (10:42)

Preview

Here is the word *dove* in four different typefaces.

dove *dove* dove **dove**

What is a *typeface*, do you think? ⚷

First view

In this part of the meeting Sue and Andrea present their market research findings to Chris. Watch and answer these two questions.

1 From Leapfrog's research, do Andrea and Sue think it would be too risky to change the name from Galaxy to Dove? How do you know what their opinion is?
2 Does Chris decide to make the change in name? ⚷

Second view

Watch again and correct these sentences.

1 Dove has a light side which is very masculine.
2 Dove has a dark side which is about softness and smoothness.
3 People felt the typeface on the packaging was quite light.
4 The image the word *dove* gives is very different to the Galaxy imagery. 🔑

Language work

Find adjectives or expressions which are opposite in meaning to those listed below. Some are in the videoscript, others you will need to find for yourself. For example:

feminine
masculine

1 light (weight) ....   4 soft (voice) ....
2 light (colour) ....   5 smooth (texture) ....
3 soft (texture) ....   6 relaxed .... 🔑

Further practice

Write a summary of Leapfrog's research findings to present to the Mars Chocolate marketing manager in the UK. Use these headings:

The name
The situation
The packaging
The name change 🔑

Remembering key vocabulary

When you have corrected your work and looked at the videoscripts for Parts
3–5, note words and expressions that are important to you in the space
provided.

nouns	verbs	other words	expressions

Revise these words and expressions later by watching these parts again and ✓
ticking the words and expressions as you hear them. Try to remember them in
their context.

4 The Solar Way

Introduction

In this sequence, you will learn about BP Solar and solar photovoltaics (the conversion of sunlight into electrical power). The sequence focuses on the production process of photovoltaic cells, the market for solar cells and their applications. It was filmed in Australia.

This sequence is especially useful if you need to describe a technical process, or define market sectors, or demonstrate applications of technology.

Read this text about BP Solar and complete the fact file.

BP Solar International (BPSI) is one of the world's largest solar power companies. For more than 15 years, the company has been a leader in the design, manufacture and supply of advanced photovoltaic power systems. A wholly-owned subsidiary of the British Petroleum Company, BP Solar now employs nearly 500 staff world-wide.

The company's Global Headquarters and its Technology Centres are located in the UK. Major manufacturing and marketing units in Spain and Australia are supplemented by joint venture companies in India, Saudi Arabia and Thailand.

Fact file: BP Solar

BP

Founded: ....

HQ: ....

Manufacturing units: ....

Joint ventures: ....

No. of employees: ....

The sequence lasts 12 minutes and is organized like this:

Part 1   Beginnings (00:04)

Preview

Check the meaning and pronunciation of these words in your dictionary.

solar   remote   watt

Viewing task

Ken Brown, General Manager at BP Solar Australia in Sydney, talks about the beginnings of solar technology. Watch and answer these questions.

1 When did solar power start?
2 Why was it developed?
3 What did a unit cost then?
   .... per watt
4 What does it cost today? .... per watt

Part 2   How solar technology works (01:04)

2.1 The solar cell (01:14)

Preview

What do you think a "solar cell" is? Choose one of these answers.

A a material which takes in sunlight and stores it as energy
B a device which converts sunlight into electrical energy
C the process which converts sunlight into electrical energy

Viewing task

Alistair Mitchell, a production controller, talks about the materials used to produce solar cells. Watch and complete these sentences.

1 Most solar cells are based on ....
2 This material looks .... but in fact it
  is ....
3 BP Solar uses .... crystal wafers.
4 A crystal wafer .... electricity on its own.

Language work

Look at these sentences from the videoscript and answer the questions.

If I put this wafer down here and get a pen and press it hard in the centre, in theory I should get four separate pieces.
If you take a silicon wafer like this and put it out in sunlight, it'll just get hot.

Which tense does Alistair use in the part of the sentence with *if*?

Which modal verbs does he use in the parts without *if*?

Which modal verb does he use when he is sure of what will happen?
Which does he use when he is not sure?

Complete these sentences with the correct form of the verb in brackets, with the correct modal verb where necessary.

1 This .... (*become*) a gas if you ....
  (*heat*) it.
2 If you .... (*not process*) the silicon wafer,
  it .... (*not produce*) electricity.
3 If we .... (*test*) everything by computer, in theory we
  .... (*not make*) any mistakes.
4 This product .... (*sell*) very well, if we
  .... (*believe*) the market research, but we can't be
  completely sure.
5 You .... (*get*) more power if you
  .... (*use*) a large wafer.
6 If we .... (*develop*) this technology,
  we .... (*save*) a lot of energy, we hope.

2.2 The production process (02:16)

Preview

Match the words on the left with the definitions on the right.

1	texturization	A	a closed system of wires through which electricity flows
2	enhance	B	a large number of solar cells grouped together
3	absorption	C	the process of changing a surface so that it is not smooth
4	current	D	to make certain
5	ensure	E	a flow of electricity through a wire
6	solar panel	F	the process of something being taken in by something else
7	circuit	G	to improve

This is a fairly technical section. Watch it without the sound. What do you think is happening? Which words from the list above can you relate to what is shown?

First view

Alistair Mitchell explains how solar cells are produced. Watch this part and number these steps as you see them. Then match pictures A–E with the steps.

	Step	Picture
clean the wafers	☐	☐
give the wafers photovoltaic ability	☐	☐
test the wafers	☐	☐
texturize the wafers	☐	☐
make the surfaces positive and negative	☐	☐

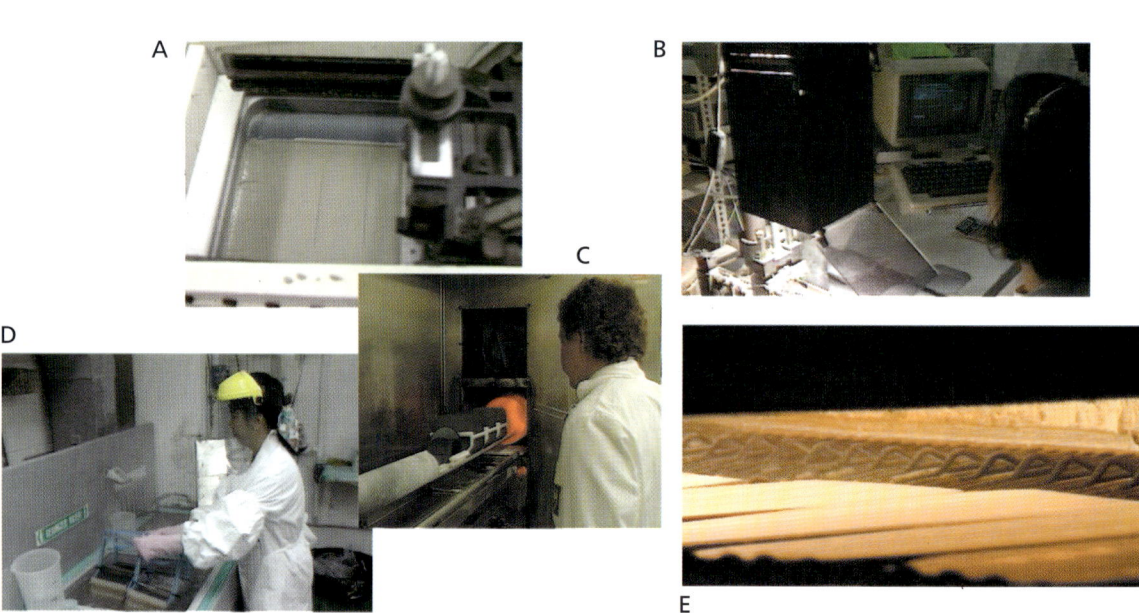

Second view

Watch again. Match these procedures to a step in the production process.

1 The wafers are heated to 1000° C.
2 The wafers are exposed to a special gas.
3 Metal contacts are printed onto the surface of the wafers.
4 The surface of the wafer is treated to increase the light absorption.

Language work

The passive voice is sometimes used to describe technical processes.
It is formed with the verb *to be* and a past participle. For example:

The silicon wafer *is texturized*.

Look at the videoscript on page 76 and underline all the verbs.
Which ones are in the passive voice?

Write a paragraph describing this process or a process known to you.
Use expressions like:

The first/next/last step is to ...   This step is called ...   Then ...

Further practice

Watch again from 02:40 and complete this sentence in which Alistair describes the process of texturization.

> ... what this does is to enhance light absorption. The more ^{1} .... you get into a solar cell, the more ^{2} .... and ^{3} .... you get out.

Watch again from 02:49 and complete this sentence in which Alistair defines "photovoltaic ability".

> The next step is to give it its photovoltaic ability. ^{4} .... the ^{5} .... to ^{6} .... sunlight directly into electricity.

Remembering key vocabulary

When you have corrected your work and looked at the videoscripts for Parts 1 and 2, note words and expressions that are important to you in the space provided.

nouns	verbs	other words	expressions

Revise these words and expressions later by watching these parts again and ✓ ticking the words and expressions as you hear them. Try to remember them in their context.

Part 3 The market (04:49)

Preview

Check the meaning of these words in your dictionary. Then use them in the sentences below.

sector	kit
grid	to pump
rural	navigation
infrastructure	

1 Everything you need to make your own radio is in this ....
2 The .... here is quite good, although the roads are in poor condition.
3 Our house is not connected to the .... because it is 30 kilometres from the nearest town.
4 We need electricity to .... the water from the river into the fields.
5 Our .... of the economy has grown fast in the last two years.
6 Transport can be a problem for people who live in .... areas.
7 The .... of large ships is now partly controlled by computers.

What do you think BP Solar's main market sectors are?

First view

Ken Brown explains how BP Solar organizes its business into four main sectors. Watch this section and complete the first line of the chart.

1	business area	....	grid-connect*	....	....
2	applications	....		....	....
3	regions		....	....	....

*Grid-connect: This sector specializes in applications which are connected to a country's national grid. These range from central power generating systems to photovoltaics which are integrated into the fronts of commercial buildings or onto the roofs of houses. The main benefit of these systems is that they reduce the demand on the local electricity grid and so reduce pollution.

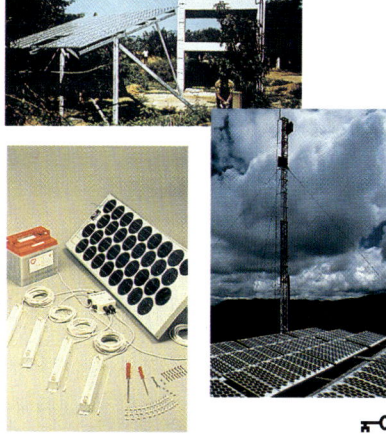

Second view

Watch again. Put these applications in the correct sector in the chart.

1 navigation systems
2 water pumping systems
3 telecommunications
4 lighting kits   ⚷O

Third view

Watch again. Fill in the regions in the chart.   ⚷O

Remembering key vocabulary

When you have corrected your work and looked at the videoscript for Part 3, note words and expressions that are important to you in the space provided.

nouns	verbs	other words	expressions

Revise these words and expressions later by watching this part again and ✓ ticking the words and expressions as you hear them. Try to remember them in their context.

Part 4   Four applications of the technology (06:21)

4.1 The Peters ice cream trolley (06:31)

Preview

Check the meaning of the following words in your dictionary.

to charge up   battery   the mains

Watch this part without the sound. What do you think is the application of solar technology in this situation?

Viewing task

Watch Richard Collins, a marketing manager, talking about the ice cream trolley and answer these questions.

1 What business sector does the ice cream trolley come under?
2 What does the solar technology allow the ice cream seller to do?
3 Is the solar panel the only source of electricity on the ice cream trolley?

4.2 The Malaysian project (07:21)

Preview

Read the sentences and answer the question.

There will be *logistical* difficulties in getting people to and from the hotel as public transport is limited and they are all arriving at different times. We will need to organize people to meet them at the airport and take them to the hotel.

Choose the best answer.

Logistical means:

A related to money
B related to organization
C related to transport

What kind of problems will BP have installing solar technology in the remote tropical area shown by the red arrow?

Viewing task

Ken Brown and a colleague discuss a rural infrastructure project in Malaysia. Watch their discussion about the transportation of the products and complete the sentences.

BP Solar will use [1] .... transportation, [2] .... and [3] .... , and if necessary, [4] .... In mountainous terrain, near the border, they will use [5] .... The project will take about [6] .... months to install.

Language work

Watch again from 07:45 and complete Ken's two questions.

What have we [1] .... [2] .... [3] .... [4] .... at this point in time?

How are we [5] .... to [6] .... this?

Now answer these questions.

Which syllables are stressed most in Ken's questions? Underline them.

Is the intonation in each question rising ⬐ or falling ⬏ ?

Repeat the questions to yourself, paying particular attention to the stress and intonation.

4.3 The Homebush Bay project (08:11)

Preview

remediated waste site = a waste area which is being made useful again
solar array = a number of solar panels connected together

What urban applications can you think of for BP solar technology?

Check the meaning of the following words and expression in your dictionary.

excess   nutrient   environmentally friendly

Match the words and expressions with the definitions on the right.

1 excess	A a substance that nourishes
2 nutrient	B not harmful to the natural world
3 to fertilize	C more than is needed
4 environmentally friendly	D to improve the quality of land

First view

Watch Tony Stocken, the business manager for special products, talking about a water pumping system supplied to the Waste Service. Answer the question and complete the sentence.

1 Where is the Homebush Bay project?
2 The client wanted the system to be
   .... from the grid and
   .... friendly.

Second view

Watch again and label the diagram.

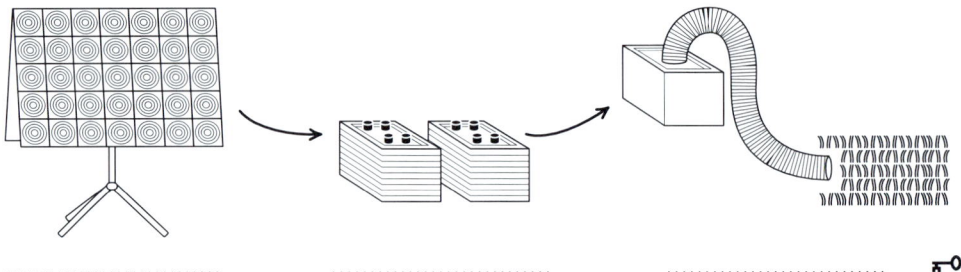

....   🔑

4.4 **The Hawkesbury River House** (9:21)

Preview

Watch this section without the sound. Why and how is solar technology used in this house, do you think?

Check the meaning of the following words and phrases in your dictionary and then use them to complete the sentences below.

generator
mod cons
hybrid
back-up

1 Our house is very comfortable because it has all the ....
2 When you use a computer, always copy your work onto another disk as a ....
3 We have our own .... because the power from the grid is not very reliable.
4 This is a kind of .... system because it uses water from the mains and rain water.   🔑

First view

Listen and complete the sentences.

1 A basic system costs about $ ....
2 A more sophisticated system costs about $ ....
3 This is a .... system. The solar system is backed up by a ....   🔑

Second view

Watch again and answer the questions.

1 Why did the home-owner decide to use solar energy?
2 Which appliances does the home-owner mention? Tick the boxes.

Washing machine ☐
Dryer ☐
TV ☐
Computer ☐
Fridge ☐
Microwave ☐
Hi-fi ☐
Hairdryer ☐   🔑

Part 5 The future for solar energy (10:48)

Preview

How do you see the future for solar energy? Make some predictions.

gidget = a slang word for *product*

First view

In which order does Ken Brown talk about three potential markets for the future?

consumer products ☐
the developed countries ☐
the developing countries ☐   🔑

Second view

Watch again and complete these notes.

1 Solar power will be the ideal source for providing .... to people in developing countries.
2 In developed countries solar panels will become a .... material.
3 When you build a house, the walls and roof will generate power, possibly feeding back into a .... or ....   🔑

Language work

Look at the words in the chart and notice how the stressed syllable of each is shown by a larger box. Put the words in the list in the correct column in the chart.

transportation	property	absorption	remote
current	process	circuit	surface
ensure	ability	logistical	convert (verb)
energy	efficient		

■ ▪	■ ▪ ▪	▪ ■	▪■▪	▪ ■ ▪ ▪	▪ ▪ ■ ▪
solar	silicon	enhance	develop	technology	application

Learning strategy

When you note a new word, mark the stressed syllable on it.

Follow-up

Write a paragraph for a report on the uses of solar energy in the 21st century. Include your own ideas and those mentioned by Ken Brown.

Think about:

– the development of solar technology (why is this necessary?)
– the manufacture of solar technology (where will this be?)
– new uses for solar energy
– the use of solar power for transport

Use words such as *will*, *may*, *might*, *could* and *probably*.

Remembering key vocabulary

When you have corrected your work and looked at the videoscripts for Parts 4 and 5, note words and expressions that are important to you in the space provided.

nouns	verbs	other words	expressions

Revise these words and expressions later by watching these parts again and ✓ ticking the words and expressions as you hear them. Try to remember them in their context.

Answer key with videoscripts

Welcome to Prince

Part 1 An overview of the company

Introduction

1 What does Prince make?
2 Where are their headquarters?
3 Where are their products made?

1.1 The products

Viewing task

1 Prince is a *major* racket company.
2 Prince makes tennis, badminton and squash rackets, *apparel*, *footwear* and accessories.
3 Most of their racket manufacturing is done in mainland China *and Taiwan*.

Videoscript

CHARLIE PEIFER: Prince is a major racket goods sporting company. We make tennis, squash, badminton rackets, apparel and footwear. We also sell the accessories to those products which would include strings and grips and sport bags and other accessory products as well. Most of our manufacturing is done in mainland China and in Taiwan. That's where the majority of rackets are manufactured today.

Further practice

Example answer

Office Maker is an Australian office furniture company. We make desks, chairs, computer workstations and filing cabinets. We also sell office accessories such as desk lamps and deskside bins. All our products are designed in Australia but most of our manufacturing is done in Indonesia, using quality local materials.

1.2 Location

Preview

1 B;   2 C;   3 D;   4 A

First view

Map A

Second view

Treviso, Italy and Singapore.

Videoscript

CHARLIE PEIFER: Prince is headquartered in Bordentown, New Jersey, which is just a little bit south of Trenton, New Jersey, and just a little bit north of Philadelphia. We also have offices in Europe, in Treviso, Italy. We have an office in Singapore which coordinates the Asian theatre for us. And then we have distributors scattered throughout the world.

1.3 Ownership

Preview

1 responsible for; 2 is comprised of; 3 acquired; 4 connects;
5 column; 6 acquire

Viewing task

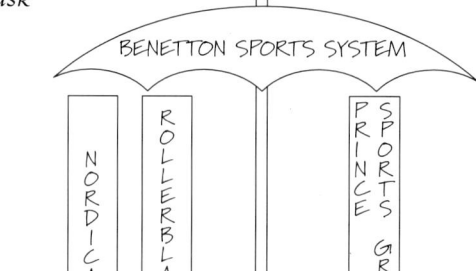

Videoscript

CHARLIE PEIFER: In 1989 we were acquired by the Benetton Sports System. Benetton Sports System is comprised of a number of different companies but an easy illustration would be to think of an umbrella and the umbrella would be the Benetton Sports System. Underneath the umbrella would be three columns: one column would be Rollerblade which is the In–Line skating company; another column would be Nordica which is the winter sport group; and the third column would be Prince Sports Group, which is our company, which deals with the summer sport goods. And then they are all connected across the bottom by Benetton Sports System Active who is responsible for the apparel across all three of those groups.

Language work

1 All our goods are designed by tennis players.
2 Our work in Asia is coordinated by our office in Singapore.
3 Our headquarters were designed by an American company.
4 Today's meeting was organized by the director.

Further practice

Example answer

Benetton Sports System is comprised of four companies: Nordica, Rollerblade, Prince Sports Group and Benetton Sports System Active. Nordica deals with winter sports equipment and Prince Sports Group with summer equipment. Rollerblade is the In-Line skating company. These three companies are like three columns which are connected by Benetton Sports System Active. This company is responsible for the clothing in all three groups.

Part 2 Dealing with the public

First view

She is polite, friendly and very clear, which makes you think she is good at her job.

Second view

1 Dealing with the public.
2 – educating consumers about *how to use* our products.
  – telling them about the *type of products* that we sell.
  – handling warranty *complaints*.

Videoscript

DAWN SMITH: Prince Sports Group Customer Services – this is Dawn.
DAWN SMITH: Hi. Would you like us to send you a catalogue?
DAWN SMITH: May I have your name and address?
DAWN SMITH: And your address?
DAWN SMITH: And what city?
DAWN SMITH: And the zip?
DAWN SMITH: OK, would you be interested in an Ektelon catalogue or Prince? Tennis or racketball?
DAWN SMITH: OK, great. My name is Dawn. I'm in the Customer Service Department. I'll get that catalogue out to you right away. If you have any questions, please call back and I'll be glad to talk to you about our products.
DAWN SMITH: Thanks.
DAWN SMITH: Bye.

DAWN SMITH: I just love dealing with the public. They call in asking about our products. We educate consumers about how to use our products. We also, um, tell them about the type of products that we sell. We handle warranty complaints, if there are any complaints about our products.

Language work

1 Hi. *Would you like us to send you* a catalogue? (*establishing a need*)
2 *May I have* your name and address? (*getting key information*)
3 OK, *would you be interested in* an Ektelon catalogue or Prince? (*getting key information*)
4 *I'll get* that catalogue out to you right away. (*confirming*)
5 If you have any questions, please call back and *I'll be glad to talk to you* about our products. (*closing the conversation*)

Further practice

Example dialogue

DAWN SMITH: Prince Sports Group Customer Services – this is Dawn.
CALLER: *Hi Dawn, I'm interested in the prices of some sports equipment.*
DAWN SMITH: Hi. Would you like us to send you a catalogue?
CALLER: *Yes, thanks, that would be great.*
DAWN SMITH: May I have your name and address?
CALLER: *My name's Jerome Allgood.*
DAWN SMITH: And your address?
CALLER: *226 Dryden Avenue.*
DAWN SMITH: And what city?
CALLER: *Trenton.*
DAWN SMITH: And the zip?
CALLER: *08638.*
DAWN SMITH: OK, would you be interested in an Ektelon catalogue or Prince? Tennis or racketball?
CALLER: *I'd like the Prince tennis one, please.*
DAWN SMITH: OK, great. My name is Dawn. I'm in the Customer Service Department. I'll get that catalogue out to you right away. If you have any questions, please call back and I'll be glad to talk to you about our products.
CALLER: *Great.*
DAWN SMITH: Thanks.
CALLER: *Thank you. Bye.*
DAWN SMITH: Bye.

Part 3 Product innovation

long body rackets	3
oversized heads on rackets	1
wide body rackets	2

Second view

1 True.
2 False. Howard Head designed the oversized-head racket in the mid-seventies.
3 True.
4 False. It gives you five: more power, control, spin, reach and comfort.
5 True.

Videoscript

DAVE HOLLAND: Well, tennis equipment has changed considerably in the last 20 years. If we go back to before 1976, really most players were playing with wooden rackets. And you notice the wood rackets' very small head sizes. Howard Head came along and not only innovated the ski industry with the first metal ski but innovated the tennis industry with the first dimensional change in tennis rackets. And that essentially means he invented the oversized head and, if you compare that to a wooden racket, you can see quite clearly you've got a much larger head in the oversize racket. That happened in the mid-seventies.

Then the next major innovation occurred with another dimensional change in the rackets which was the wide body, and wide bodies allowed for greater stiffness in rackets, therefore producing much more power.

And today the next biggest innovation is also dimensional and that is length. Here is our new Mach 1000. The Prince Long Body racket gives you five major benefits. They are: more power, more control, more spin, more reach and more comfort.

Well, I think this is the, this is the last dimensional change in a racket that can occur. Again, just to repeat, you had the first dimensional change which was head size – larger head size; the second dimensional change was, was cross-section and now we're looking at the third and final area that you can change in terms of a racket's geometry, which is length. So I think what you'll see over the next several years is who can make the best longer rackets.

Language work

1 has changed;   2 were playing (*played* is also possible);   3 came;   4 happened;
5 was;   6 gives

Further practice

Example answer

The telephone has changed dramatically in the past 60 years, especially since the late 1980s and during the 1990s. In 1937 the 300 desk model had a bell in its base, instead of separately on the wall.

  In the 1950s coloured telephones became popular in the home. In 1968 the "trimline" telephone was introduced with major dimensional changes. This phone also replaced the dial with push buttons. The next major innovation came in the late 1980s with the introduction of the cordless phone and the mobile phone. People were able to telephone direct from their cars using mobile phones. In the late 1990s mobile phone technology is moving fast. Enormous dimensional change has occurred. Some telephones are now roughly the same size as a business card. Mobiles run on batteries and have many special features, for example, "caller identity" that allows you to see the number of the person calling you before you answer. A recent development is the interface between the mobile and the personal computer. With a data card, you can receive information from a PC and surf the Internet. Who knows what the phone of 2010 will be like?

Part 4 Tele-sales to retailers

Preview

1 A; 2 C

First view

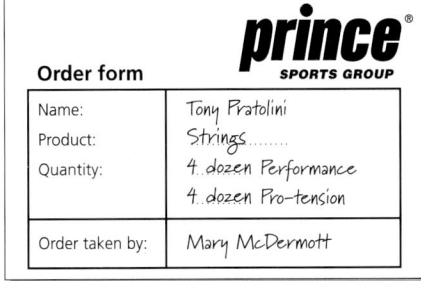

Order form

Name:	Tony Pratolini
Product:	Strings........
Quantity:	4 dozen Performance
	4 dozen Pro-tension
Order taken by:	Mary McDermott

Second view

1 Tony; 2 Mary; 3 Tony; 4 Tony; 5 Mary; 6 Tony

Videoscript

MARY McDERMOTT: Hi. Is Tony in?

TONY: Speaking.

MARY McDERMOTT: Tony. It's Mary from Prince. How are you?

TONY: Fine. And yourself?

MARY McDERMOTT: Not too bad. How was your holiday weekend?

TONY: Oh, great. How was yours?

MARY McDERMOTT: Good. Thank you very much. Listen, the reason I'm calling you today is to make sure, one, you received the catalogue and selection cards that I sent out to you.

TONY: Certainly did.

MARY McDERMOTT: ... and, two, I wanted to let you know, since you do have a very good stringing business that we have some overgrips on close-outs.

TONY: Which ones?

MARY McDERMOTT: It's the Superdry Overgrip – the pricing originally was $38 a dozen but based on the colour right now it can range anywhere from $12.50 a dozen to $7 a dozen. Do you ...?

TONY: What are the prices on the different colours?

MARY McDERMOTT: OK ... in black it would be 12.50. In the emerald green colour it will $8. In hot pink it would be $7 and in the dark purple it would be $8 also.

TONY: OK.

MARY McDERMOTT: I'm also running a special on the Mono rackets this month. If you buy the Adult 650 for regular dealer cost, you get the Junior Precision Mono at no charge.

TONY: That's a pretty good deal.

MARY McDERMOTT: Yeah, it's not bad for this time of the year. Is there anything I can get you today?

TONY: Yeah, I need some sets of strings.

MARY McDERMOTT: OK. How many dozen did you want?

TONY: Four of the Performance and the Pro-tension.

MARY McDERMOTT: Four of each?

TONY: Yeah.

MARY McDERMOTT: That'll be fine.

TONY: Thanks.

MARY McDERMOTT: OK. I'll give you a call in a couple of weeks to check in again.

TONY: Take care.

MARY McDERMOTT: You too. Bye bye.

Language work

Stage 1: How are you?

Stage 2: Listen, the reason I'm calling you today is ...

Stage 3: OK, I'll give you a call in a couple of weeks to check in again.

Part 5 Design and testing

Preview

The colour

First view

C. (It ensures an adequate fit of plastic parts with frames.)

Second view

A. (In four ways: power, vibration, comfort and control.)

Videoscript

SUSAN MAC: Yes, hello Vicky. It's Sue. The green. It's a little off so I need to get another sample made. I'm going to fax you over some drawings.

SUSAN MAC: Yeah. Hm mm. OK. Well, if we can get it sent out by Friday, that's when we really need it by. So actually as soon as you can. That would be great.

SUSAN MAC: Thanks. Bye.

BRIAN BLONSKI: We use computer-aided design to document the shape of all of our products and to ensure an adequate fit of plastic parts with frames. Our latest innovation is the long body racket in which we've created a new technology, using advanced materials and design evolutions, to make the game easier to play.

BRIAN BLONSKI: We spend a great deal of time testing product in the laboratory. In fact, we have developed tests which are capable of predicting the product's performance on court in terms of power, in terms of vibration, comfort, control.

Further practice

Call from Sue

Problem with the green.

*She needs another sample
sent out by Friday.*

She will fax some drawings.

Part 6 A retail customer comes to visit

Viewing task

1 At two o'clock.
2 Yes, she does. He says, "It's good to have you back."
3 Yes, she has. He says, "So it's been a while since you've been here."
4 The new line.
5 He has a bigger office.

Videoscript

JEANNETTE: Good afternoon. I'm Jeannette Samuels and I'm here to see Bob Fenton for a two o'clock appointment.

RECEPTIONIST: OK. Would you please sign our book? And you can have a seat. And I will let him know you're here. Bob Fenton, please call the front desk. Bob Fenton, please call the front desk.

BOB: Jeannette. How are you?
JEANNETTE: Fine. How are you doing?
BOB: I'm doing very well. Welcome to Prince Sports Group.
JEANNETTE: Thank you.
BOB: It's really good to see you.
JEANNETTE: Nice to see you.

BOB: Yeah, it's good to have you back.

JEANNETTE: Thank you.

BOB: Why don't we walk over to my office and we'll get a chance to go through the line a little bit?

JEANNETTE: Wonderful. That sounds great.

BOB: Great.

BOB: Come on in the office, Jeannette.

JEANNETTE: Thank you.

BOB: Why don't you sit right here? And let me take your coat.

JEANNETTE: Thank you.

BOB: So it's been a while since you've been here.

JEANNETTE: I know. Things have changed.

BOB: Sure have. Actually they gave me a bigger office so things must be doing ...

JEANNETTE: I noticed.

BOB: Yeah, things are doing well.

BOB: So, Jeannette, er, let me show you some of the reasons, I guess, for our success. Er, I think most have really stemmed from the three new introductions that you have in your stores right now. The Mach 1000, the Extender Ripstick and the Precision Michael Chang Autograph ...

Language work

1 Why don't we ...?
2 Wonderful. That sounds great.
3 let me ...
4 Welcome to ... , it's really good to see you, it's good to have you back
5 Let me
6 Why don't we, Wonderful. That sounds great.
7 It's (really) good to see you.

Part 7 Company culture

7.1 The dress code

Viewing task

1 According to Charlie Peifer, the business culture in the US – and around the world – is changing *rapidly*.
2 According to Charlie Peifer, smart clothes *don't necessarily* make people work better.
3 Rick Margin says you can wear any *Benetton Sports System clothing* at Prince.
4 Rick Margin says people who come to Prince say it must be *wonderful* to be able to dress casually.
5 The casual dress code *isn't the defining reason* for working at Prince.

Videoscript

CHARLIE PEIFER: The business culture in the US – and I think around the world – is changing rapidly. There was a time when people had to wear white shirts and stiff collars and neck ties. And what we found is that doesn't necessarily make you a better workforce.

RICK MARGIN: Well, the policy actually is you have to wear, um, Benetton Sports System apparel. It's casual, it's relaxed. It looks good from the outside. When people come in, they say it must be wonderful to be casual all the time and to wear this wonderful ... these great warm-ups and neat footwear coming to work. "This is the way I'd like to work." It's not a defining reason why you would work at Prince.

Language work

Example sentences

When Tom started work on the factory floor of a South Korean company in Britain, he had to wear protective clothing. He also had to start work at 7.00 a.m. Today Tom has to wear a suit and tie. He also has to visit South Korea regularly.

7.2 *The working atmosphere*

Preview

1 enjoyable;   2 youthful;   3 intimate;   4 fun

Viewing task

1 The relaxed environment.
2 Knowing who to speak to and what the system was.
3 Get the job done.
4 He plays less than before he came to Prince.
5 A love of the sports.
6 Being able to relate to and try out the product.

Videoscript

BRIAN BLONSKI: It is a relaxed environment and that is, I think, a very positive thing. I used to work for a much larger corporation, in fact about 20 times the size of Prince, and it was very difficult to know who to speak with to get your answer and what the system was in order to go through a ... a complete development. With Prince being much smaller, more intimate and more youthful in terms of the employees, it's very easy to get your job done.

RICK MARGIN: I play less tennis today than I did before I came to Prince. We work hard here. But the one thing that collectively brings us together is we've got a love for the sports that we're involved. It's a fun environment to work in.

BRIAN BLONSKI: Well, I joined Prince four years ago and I think the most enjoyable part about my job is the ability to relate to the product. It's something that you can design and develop and have in your hand in a period of five to six months and actually go out onto the court and feel how good of a job you did.

SEQUENCE 2   The Delivery

Introduction

In fact, speed of delivery, quality, freshness and reliability are major concerns for this company.

Part 1   The order

Preview

1 deliver;   2 top-up;   3 includes;   4 promotion;   5 pick up

First view

1 30 by 10 by 2 (which means 30 bags which contain 10 two-kilo bags).
2 No, she isn't. (She'll need to check with the factory.)
3 Tonight.
4 A top-up.
5 The packaging factory (Kroonton) and the transportation company (de Koeijer).

Second view

Example dialogue

CAROLINE: Hello.
FREDERIC: *Is that Caroline?*
CAROLINE: Yes, speaking.
FREDERIC: *Hello, this is Frederic.*
CAROLINE: Oh, good morning, Frederic. How are you?

FREDERIC: *Fine. And you?*

CAROLINE: Not too bad, thank you.

FREDERIC: *Good. We need another 30 by 10 by 2 bags to go down to Lièvin tonight.*

CAROLINE: Right. 30 by 10 by 2. OK. I'm not actually in the office yet. I shall be there within about half an hour. Could I call you then after I've checked with the factory?

FREDERIC: *Sure.*

CAROLINE: OK, then. Fine. I'll call you back.

FREDERIC: *Thanks.*

CAROLINE: All right. Bye for now.

Videoscript

CAROLINE: Hello.

CAROLINE: Yes, speaking.

CAROLINE: Oh, good morning Frederic. How are you?

CAROLINE: Not too bad, thank you.

CAROLINE: Right. 30 by 10 by 2. OK. I'm not actually in the office yet. I shall be there within about half an hour. Could I call you then after I've checked with the factory?

CAROLINE: OK, then. Fine. I'll call you back.

CAROLINE: All right. Bye for now.

CAROLINE: I had a call from Auchan just as I was leaving the house. Frederic wants another 30 by 10 by 2 kilos to go down to Lièvin tonight. Do you think we've still got time to meet the lorry? I'm not quite sure what time it's leaving Yerseke.

CHRIS: Well, firstly is this part of a promotion or, or is this a top-up?

CAROLINE: I think it's an ordinary pro ... , ordinary delivery that they haven't included in their first lot of orders.

CHRIS: Well, it's a bit late. Um, can you get on to Jap at Kroonton to see whether he's got time to pack them or not?

REBECCA: Yeah.

CHRIS: And then you'll speak to Eric at de Koeijer's to see if he can pick it up and deliver it on time, will you?

REBECCA: Yup. Yup. OK. Will do.

Language work

1 <u>a</u>ctually
2 with<u>in</u>
3 pro<u>mo</u>tion
4 <u>or</u>dinary
5 de<u>li</u>very
6 I'm <u>not</u> actually in the <u>office</u> <u>yet</u>.
7 I'll <u>call</u> you <u>back</u>.
8 <u>Well</u>, it's a <u>bit</u> <u>late</u>.

Part 2 About Seafare

First view

Diagram C

Second view

1 Ireland, Wales, Scotland, Holland, France and Spain.
2 France, Spain, Italy, Belgium and Holland.

Videoscript

CAROLINE: Seafare bases itself in the middle if you like. It acts as a coordinating base for the people who supply it with its products and the people who are going to use those products, who are going to buy them. We are liaising if you like between the fishermen who are fishing products and looking for markets and the people who want to buy the products and find and source the products. We are doing two jobs, one at each end.

CHRIS: When we started, almost everything we were selling was to Spain. We have visited hundreds and hundreds of different buyers and we have evolved a system of generally buying from people who farm their mussels so that we've got regularity of supply and a good quality for the customers.

   Mostly we're buying, from here, we're buying from Ireland and from Wales and Scotland. We're also buying from Holland, France and Spain. We're selling to France, to Spain, to Italy, to Belgium and Holland.

Language work

Example answer

Sun Fruit *supplies* a variety of tropical fruit to European supermarkets. It is a large company which *liaises* between fruit growers who *are looking for* markets, and supermarkets who need someone to *source* the fruit. It *has evolved* a system of transporting fruit quickly and efficiently.

Part 3 Dealing with the order

Preview

Platform in this context means a "depot" or a "hub" where the product is delivered for redistribution to the supermarkets.

Viewing task

Example answer

> Dear Jap
> This is to confirm our order for 30 bags of ten two-kilo bags of mussels for the Auchan Lièvin platform.
> Thanks very much for processing this last-minute order.
>
> Best wishes
> Rebecca

Videoscript

JAP: Kroonton. Good morning.
REBECCA: Oh, hello Jap. It's Rebecca here.
REBECCA: OK, thanks. And you?
REBECCA: Good, good. Um, I'm ringing you because we've just had a last-minute addition to the orders for Auchan. It's for the Lièvin platform. And they'd like another 30 by 10 by 2 bags.
JAP: So they want an extra 30 bags. Yeah.
REBECCA: Right, I'll, I'll send you through a fax to confirm that then.
REBECCA: OK. Thank you. Thanks. Bye bye.
JAP: Thank you. Bye. Bye.

Language work

1 It's;   2 here;   3 ringing you because;   4 Right;
5 send you through a fax

Part 4 Sourcing and Quality

4.1 Dutch mussels

Preview

Process		Picture
1	collection from seabed	C
2	landing	A
3	moving by conveyor belt	E
4	selection	B
5	packing	D

Viewing task

1 Into larger and smaller mussels.
2 The smaller ones.
3 3000.

Videoscript

CHRIS: Here we're in the port of Yerseke in Holland. This is the centre of the Dutch industry. Here the mussels are divided into the larger and the smaller mussels and we pack the smaller mussels here for the French market. This year we'll move about 3000 tons of mussels.

4.2 Purification and Grading

First view

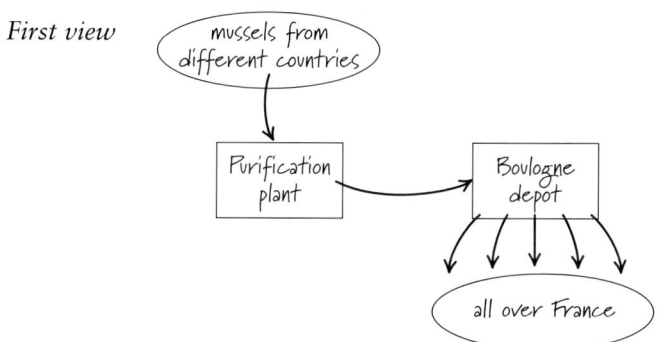

Second view

Grade A classification: You can eat the mussels *directly from the sea.*
Grade B classification: The mussels need to *be purified.*
Grade C classification: The mussels need twice *the length of purification as Grade B ones.*

Videoscript

CHRIS: We're in the purification station at Wimereux in France just ten minutes outside of Boulogne. And this is where the mussels that come from Ireland, other parts of France, Wales and Scotland, come here to be purified.

CHRIS: Once they're purified, we take them the short journey to Boulogne where there is a transport depot and we can ship them anywhere throughout France depending on which transporter we use.

CHRIS: Some we bring here just for packing. They come from waters that are classified A. The whole of the coastline is divided into classifications. A classification: you can eat the mussels directly from the sea. B classification: they need to come here for purification. C grade: they must endure intensive purification which is basically purification for twice the length of time but we don't take mussels from grade C waters anyway.

Part 5　Arranging transportation

Viewing task

1 The weekend.
2 The departure time of the lorry.
3 To send him a fax to confirm the order (for Auchan).
4 She tells Caroline everything is organized.
5 To ring Frederic.
6 To confirm the order is being processed.

Videoscript

REBECCA: Oh, hello. Is that Eric?
REBECCA: Yes, hello Eric, it's Rebecca here from Seafare.
REBECCA: OK. How are you?
REBECCA: You have a nice weekend?
REBECCA: Good. Good.
REBECCA: OK. I've just spoken to Jap at Kroonton to increase our order for Auchan. I've got another 30 bags to be delivered to Lièvin. What time is your lorry actually leaving?
REBECCA: Oh, right, right. That's fine then. So Jap should have them ready by then without any problems.
REBECCA: OK. Right, OK. I'll send you through a fax to confirm then.
REBECCA: Bye bye.

REBECCA: Um, Caroline?
CAROLINE: Yes.
REBECCA: Right, I've spoken to Jap and to de Koeijer and there's no problem for the extra 30 bags.
CAROLINE: Oh, fine. OK.
REBECCA: So de Koeijer is loading at three o'clock or so.
CAROLINE: Right.
REBECCA: So it's all going ahead.
CAROLINE: Thank you very much. Give Frederic a ring.

Language work

Sentence 1 talks about future actions that have already been planned.
Sentence 2 talks about future actions that have not already been planned.

1 will leave / 'll leave;　2 are going / 're going;　3 is spending / 's spending;
4 will phone / 'll phone;　5 will discuss / 'll discuss, will call / 'll call

Part 6　Transportation

6.1 Choosing the route

Preview

1 C;　2 A;　3 E;　4 F;　5 B;　6 D

Viewing task

Route B

Videoscript

CAROLINE: Well, it is an order which has been received at the last minute so therefore we've got little time to get it to the platform. We have two routes that we could take: we could either go by road all the way via Antwerp or we could take a ferry and cut the corner going via Zelzate and then onto the motorway at Ghent.

CAROLINE: The lorry will be leaving at about three thirty and, bearing in mind that time, we're likely if we went via Antwerp to hit the rush hour traffic around Antwerp, and that would hold us up, so I think we'll choose to go on the ferry and cross-country.

Language work

1 They could either increase the price or (they could) reduce the quantity in each bag.
2 I could either write a letter or (I could) send a fax.
3 We could either deliver directly to the shops or (we could) pay for distribution.
4 He could either meet you on Wednesday or (he could) phone you this afternoon.
5 We could either get a taxi or (we could) wait for a bus.

6.2 Transportation problems

Viewing task

1 Man-made problems: *breakdowns* and *changes in a timetable*.
2 *Natural* problems: for example, *rough weather*.

Videoscript

CAROLINE: Breakdowns of course can be a big problem. Ferries: a change in a timetable can cause us problems. Rough weather of course would delay us. So we're faced with man-made problems and natural problems.

6.3 Delivery to the supermarkets

Viewing task

1 False. Seafare *sometimes* delivers directly to the supermarket. But it also delivers to depots.
2 True.
3 True.
4 False. *Most* (99.9 per cent) of the time Seafare delivers on time.

Videoscript

CHRIS: There are some supermarket groups to whom we deliver all of their products to their own central depot, marked up with different colours and then they take it to their regional depots. And from their regional depots small vehicles take it to the shops. On other occasions they ask us to deliver directly to the shops.

CHRIS: We've evolved from effectively being an agent of the fishermen to being somebody who is sourcing material for the supermarkets. The supermarkets in France now, they give us the orders in the early morning and we actually have to pack the mussels and put them on the lorry the same day, sometimes within about two hours of receiving the orders.

CAROLINE: We, as a company, pride ourselves in getting our goods to their destination at the right time. And 99.9 per cent of the time we do it.

Language work

1 agent;   2 destination;   3 vehicle;   4 to pride oneself;   5 regional;   6 goods;
7 order

Further practice

Example answer

Seafare is a small British company with an annual turnover of £1.5 million. Its main business is to act as a liaison between those who want to buy shellfish, mainly supermarkets in France, Spain, Italy, Belgium and Holland, and fishermen in Ireland, Wales and Scotland. They move about 3000 tons of mussels a year. The company was set up in 1988 by its two owners, Chris Phippen and Caroline Poultney.

What's in a brand name?

Part 1 Making contact

Preview

1 brief; 2 assess; 3 brand; 4 project; 5 consumers; 6 loyalists

First view

A

Second view

1 False. They do know each other. They are friendly to each other on the phone.
2 True. He says they want to "assess some consumer reaction to that change".
3 False. Chris wants to find out the opinions of both Galaxy and other chocolate eaters.
4 True. Chris and Andrea are going to meet to discuss the project on Friday.
5 False. Andrea says she will bring someone else to the meeting who will work with her on the project.
6 False. Chris wants the results of the market research within four weeks.

Videoscript

RECEPTIONIST: Leapfrog. Good afternoon.
RECEPTIONIST: Can I ask who's calling?
RECEPTIONIST: Hello, Chris. I'll try the line for you.

ANDREA: Hello.
RECEPTIONIST: It's Chris Hardy for you.
ANDREA: Hello, Chris. How are you?
CHRIS: I'm fine, thanks. How are you?
ANDREA: Very well, very well. What can we do for you?
CHRIS: Andrea, we're looking to commission some consumer research and I was hoping to, to come and talk to you about it.
ANDREA: Hmm. What are you wanting to find out?
CHRIS: Well, you probably know we've got a, the Galaxy chocolate brand here in the UK and there's a possibility that some time in the future we're going to have to change the name to Dove and therefore we'd like to assess some consumer reaction to that change.
ANDREA: Right. Um, would you keep any Galaxy branding on there at all?
CHRIS: No, certainly not in the long term. In the short term maybe.
ANDREA: Right, right. And who, who do you think we need to speak to about this? Are we talking about standard chocolate consumers?
CHRIS: Yes, all chocolate consumers but then with a particular bias towards, er, let's say 18- to 35- or 40-year-old women.
ANDREA: Uh huh. And I would have said some Galaxy loyalists and some people who are less close to it, yeah? OK. Well, I suppose what we ought to do is have a brief, a briefing meeting some time, shouldn't we?
CHRIS: Er, let me just have a look. I think towards the end of this week would be great if that's OK for you. How about something like Friday?
ANDREA: Friday. Yeah, Friday would be fine for us. Um, what I would do is, is bring someone else along who is going to work on the project with us probably. What about if we said just before lunch?
CHRIS: That sounds fine. So if, if I come to Leapfrog at eleven thirty Friday.
ANDREA: OK. And have you got any sense of timing for this?
CHRIS: Well, I'd really like to complete the research within the next four weeks.
ANDREA: Four weeks. No problem at all.

Language work

1 What can we do for you?
2 I was hoping to, to come and talk to you about it.

3 How about something like
4 Friday would be fine for us.
5 What about if we said

I was hoping, towards the end of the week, something like, would be fine, if we said. The modal used here to express possibility is *would*.

Part 2   Visiting Leapfrog

Preview

1 in detail;   2 sample;   3 disrupt;   4 recipe;   5 regular

First view

In the conversation they discuss the **recipe** for the chocolate bar (which is not changing) and Sue asks if Chris wants them to investigate the **design** (of the packaging). (He says he does, but it is not the main objective of the market research.)

Second view

1 hi;   2 kick off;   3 objectives;   4 identical;   5 quota;   6 great;   7 tie up

Videoscript

CHRIS: Andrea.
ANDREA: Hello, Chris. Come and sit down.
CHRIS: Thanks very much.
ANDREA: Um, I'll just call Sue over. I'd like you to meet her. She's going to be working on the project. Sue, do you want to come over?
CHRIS: Hi, I'm Chris Hardy. Hi.
SUE: Hi. Nice to meet you.
ANDREA: Right, well I thought, um, we should probably kick off with the objectives really.
CHRIS: OK, well really, as I was saying to you on the phone, Andrea, as you probably know, we sell Galaxy chocolate here in the UK and there's the possibility that we at some time in the future will be looking to change the name to Dove.
ANDREA: So will the product be changing at all?
CHRIS: No, the recipe won't be changing at all. It's a bit like, if you remember a few years ago we changed the name from Marathon to Snickers. So the identical recipe. We're just talking about assessing consumers' reaction to the name change.
SUE: OK, Chris. What about a sample for this project? Who are we going to be talking to?
CHRIS: Right, well, I think a little bit like Andrea and I were discussing on the phone earlier in the week, I think we're probably ... everyone should be regular eaters of chocolate, let's say people who have eaten chocolate at least once in the last four weeks. And then we want a quota of regular Galaxy eaters, maybe 50 per cent of the people to have been, to be regular Galaxy eaters.
ANDREA: Do you want us to look at the different designs, Chris?
CHRIS: That's probably a good idea. It's not a main objective of the research. But maybe without disrupting the rest of it, yes. Let's see if we can fit that in as well.
ANDREA: Great. Well, I think that just about ties it up, doesn't it? How about going off and getting some lunch and then we can talk about this in more detail afterwards?

Language work

will + infinitive: I'll just call Sue over.
will + *be* + *ing* form: we ... will be looking to change the name, So will the product be changing at all?, the recipe won't be changing at all

1 will be moving;   2 I'll come;   3 I'll look;   4 we'll be seeing;   5 we'll fax

Further practice

1 I'll just call;   2 I'd like you to;   3 do you want to come;
4 as I was saying to you on the phone;   5 I think a little bit like;

6 were discussing on the phone earlier in the week; 7 Well, I think that just about ties it up; 8 How about going off and getting

Part 3 How Leapfrog started

Viewing task

1 Leapfrog is a young company. It started in 1994.
2 They first worked from Judy's dining room.
3 They moved into offices after seven months and the company has grown quite quickly.
4 They worked together in a big market research company.
5 As well as market research, she has worked in advertising.
6 To do something for themselves, meaning to be self-employed rather than working for someone else.

Videoscript

JUDY: It was in May 1994. I'd just had my third child and we sort of set up in a dining room at my house and we were there for about seven months and then we bought some premises which are here in Windsor. In two years we've done, you know, we've grown quite quickly.

ANDREA: Well. I met Judy at the research business, which is a very large, very well established research company, market research company. Prior to that, I'd been involved in the advertising industry, so I'd worked for advertising agencies for six, seven years. And Judy and I just decided that we wanted to try and do something for ourselves and set up Leapfrog.

Part 4 The group discussions

4.1 Organizing the groups

Viewing task

Sue from Leapfrog

...Two... groups of ...women.. .
...Ten... o'clock on Tuesday ...13th.. ˙March.
At Leapfrog. for one hour to an hour and a half.

Videoscript

SUE: Hello, Eunice. Hi. It's Sue here from Leapfrog.
SUE: Hi. How are you?
SUE: Very good, thank you very much.
SUE: I was just wondering, would you be able to help us with recruiting a couple of groups of women for us?
SUE: It's on Tuesday 13th. We'll be holding the group here and it'll be at ten o'clock.
SUE: An hour, an hour and a half.

Language work

Example answers

1 I was wondering if you would have time to help me / you could help me with this report.
2 I was wondering if I could leave work early today.
3 I was wondering if you could recommend somewhere to stay in (...).
4 I was wondering if you would be able to send me some information on our new product.

4.2 Qualitative market research

Viewing task

1 informal;   2 four, eight;   3 freely, depth;   4 response;
5 conversational (meaning informal)

Videoscript

ANDREA: Well, the majority of qualitative research takes place in what we call group discussions and these
are very informal groups – quite small, between about four and eight people. What happens is people
talk quite freely and in depth about the specific topic in hand and what you can do is expose them to
particular examples of products or packaging or whatever it is and gain their response. But it's very
conversational.

4.3 A group discussion

Preview

1 packaging;   2 indulgent;   3 shelf;   4 smooth

The name

Viewing task

The interviewees associate the word *dove* with soap (because this is a brand name of a
soap in the UK), peace, the bird itself and the colour white. They expect it to be a smooth
chocolate for a relaxed and indulgent moment.

Videoscript

SUE: Thank you very much for agreeing to come along this morning. Right. I'm going to write something down
on the board and I just want you to shout out your associations with this word.
WOMAN A: Soap.
SUE: Soap.
WOMAN B: Peace.
WOMAN C: Bird.
WOMAN A: Bird.
SUE: Bird.
WOMAN B: White.
WOMAN C: White. Yup.
SUE: OK. Tell me more. What is the chocolate bar called Dove going to be like?
WOMAN B: Yeah, I would picture it as a smooth chocolate.
SUE: A smooth type of chocolate. Right.
WOMAN C: Very relaxed and very indulgent. Chewy and smooth.
SUE: Relaxed. Indulgent. OK.

The situation

Viewing task

The group say they might eat the chocolate after dinner either alone or with someone else.
It isn't a sociable type of chocolate to be eaten with a lot of other people.

Videoscript

SUE: I mean, we're just talking about relaxed and how the bar Dove would be in terms of, you know, it would
be quite a relaxed bar. It's when you're feeling indulgent. I've got a board here that has got lots of different
types of occasions on it. And I wanted you to have a look at this and tell me whether any of these
occasions seemed to fit with what you expect a Dove chocolate bar to be about.
WOMAN A: At the dinner table but not *at* the dinner table. That sort of feeling of relaxed sort of intimate
romance.
SUE: Romantic, right. Any others?

WOMAN B: If it's in an intimate, relaxed moment, you wouldn't eat it with a crowd of people.

SUE: So it's not a socializing kind of bar of chocolate. It's much more, er, an either on your own or just with one other person. OK, brilliant.

The packaging

Viewing task

Although Linda says the packaging works well, overall they are pretty negative, saying it looks cheap and the same as anything else.

Videoscript

SUE: Does this, this packaging suit the, the name Dove? Does it go with all the images that you had of, of Dove being quite relaxed and quite sensuous and smooth and indulgent?

LINDA: I think, I think it does actually. I do. I think it works very well.

SUE: Tell me why, Linda?

LINDA: To me it stands out.

SUE: OK. Do other people agree with Linda on that or not?

: I think it portrays the right image. I just think it's very similar to, you know, other colours and packaging that are on the market at the moment.

: I think the backing, the brown on the backing goes, but the writing is too hard, it's too straight.

SUE: We've got a couple of other ones here that are part of the same range. What do you think of, of these ones?

: It's just the same as everything before. I mean there's, there's so many down there that are, have got the same ... you could just take the name off and put the name Galaxy ...

: ... that's right. The name is a plain, just a chocolate bar.

: Yes, they look quite ordinary. Just like anything else on the shelf really.

SUE: Are there any of these words that seem to fit the imagery that is coming across from these packaging designs?

: Cheap.

SUE: OK, cheap.

: There's a masculinity about, about the two bottom ones.

SUE: Right.

Changing the name

Viewing task

Overall, they are positive about the name change although some people have doubts.

Videoscript

SUE: How would you feel if the name Galaxy became Dove?

: Having Galaxy going over to Dove ... I think Galaxy is such ... has been established as being such a sort of like evening um intimate sort of chocolate ...

SUE: Huh huh.

: Whereas with Dove I'd like to see having different colours, lighter colours ...

SUE: Right.

: ... more the innocent sort of chocolate.

: I think the name Dove actually suits Galaxy. If you think about Galaxy, er, just picture the chocolate and the taste, the name Dove is actually quite suitable for the type of chocolate bar that it is.

SUE: Right.

Language work

1 P;   2 P (it is very noticeable);   3 P (it gives the right impression);   4 N;   5 N

Part 5 The research findings

Preview

A *typeface* is a design of letters (and numbers) used in printing.

First view

1 No, Andrea and Sue do not think it would be too risky to change the name from Galaxy to Dove. Andrea says "we didn't believe from the research we've conducted that there is a significant worry or threat for the brand by changing the name to Dove."

2 No, Chris doesn't make any decision at all on whether to change the name or not.

Second view

1 Dove has a light side which is very *feminine.*
2 Dove has a *light* side which is about softness and smoothness.
3 People felt the typeface on the packaging was quite *heavy.*
4 The image the word Dove gives is very *similar* to the Galaxy imagery.

Videoscript

CHRIS: Exactly. I was thinking that. Just looking at your list of adjectives there, I mean a lot of them are adjectives that would appear on Galaxy, Galaxy documents.

SUE: Certainly.

ANDREA: Hmm.

SUE: Dove has a light and a dark side to it which is quite interesting. The light is all about the softness and the smoothness and it is very feminine and light and clean and it's very pure. And on the other hand there's also the darkness of it which is about the relaxedness of it really. And it's much more rich and indulgent.

ANDREA: It's quite interesting as well the way the women spontaneously talked about "this would be a chocolate like Galaxy".

SUE: Yes.

ANDREA: So they were seeing a link in terms of values ...

CHRIS: Uh huh.

ANDREA: ... over and beyond the Dove name.

CHRIS: Yup.

SUE: People immediately talked about Galaxy and recognized a similarity and really they took the cues from the brown which is a very strong Galaxy colouring. Also the typeface: people started talking about "Ah, that looks like, you know, the type of typeface that Galaxy uses".

CHRIS: Yes.

SUE: People were talking about lightening the Dove brand name because currently they felt that it was ... the typeface itself was quite heavy and masculine ...

CHRIS: Right.

SUE: ... and the name Dove actually seems quite light.

CHRIS: Mmm.

SUE: Dove should have a slight lightness and softness about it ...

CHRIS: Mmm.

SUE: ... and it did seem a little bit heavy ...

CHRIS: These were just slightly heavy, were they?

SUE: ... for some people.

CHRIS: Right.

ANDREA: One of the important elements that people did pick up was the very heavy folding of the brown silk beneath the lettering and it seemed to suggest very clearly that not only did this wrapper look like Galaxy and imply Galaxy but it was a promise that the actual product inside was really going to taste the same.

ANDREA: We would say that we didn't believe from the research that we've conducted that there is a significant worry or threat for the brand by changing the name to Dove.

SUE: And the other thing is that we feel that the image that the word *dove* portrays is very similar to the imagery that you've built up over time for the brand Galaxy so therefore you've got the synergy, um, between the old brand name and the name Dove.

CHRIS: So, thank you very much. That was excellent. I found it very interesting and of course it seems very positive so I'm very happy. Thank you.

ANDREA: Excellent. Good.

SUE: Good.

Language work

1 heavy; 2 dark; 3 hard/tough; 4 loud; 5 rough; 6 tense

Further practice

Example answer

<u>The name</u>

Although at first people associated the name with the soap of the same name, when the context of chocolate was given they thought of smoothness, and relaxed and indulgent moments.

<u>The situation</u>

They felt it was a chocolate for intimate, perhaps romantic, occasions. They would eat it alone or with one other person.

<u>The packaging</u>

Reaction to the packaging was fairly positive, but some felt it looked cheap and like other packaging. Its similarity to Galaxy was noticed.

<u>The name change</u>

Changing the name from Galaxy to Dove was generally accepted. However, some interviewees felt that Dove had lighter, softer associations that did not totally suit the Galaxy name.

SEQUENCE 4   The Solar Way

Introduction

> ### *Fact file: BP Solar*
>
> **Founded:** 15 years ago
>
> **HQ:** UK
>
> **Manufacturing units:** Spain, Australia
>
> **Joint ventures:** India, Saudi Arabia, Thailand
>
> **No. of employees:** 500

Part 1   Beginnings

Viewing task

1 In the 1970s.
2 To provide power in remote areas / areas which are far from towns and cities.
3 US $100
4 US $5

Videoscript

KEN BROWN: Solar power is a very new industry as such, and it had its basic roots in the 1970s. People recognized there was a need for power in remote areas so, building on that, we then started to use solar cells in remote applications. The cost of solar cells in the 1970s was something like 100 dollars per, per watt, if not more. Well, now the industry has been able to drive the cost down to five dollars – US dollars – per watt.

Part 2 How solar technology works

2.1 The solar cell

Preview

B

Viewing task

1 silicon;   2 boring, exciting;   3 single;   4 doesn't develop

Videoscript

ALISTAIR MITCHELL: Most of the solar cells which are sold around the world are based on silicon.

This is a silicon wafer that we use to make our solar cells. It's pretty plain and boring-looking, but it's quite an exciting material really. The silicon wafer that we use is made from single-crystal silicon which gives the wafer certain special properties. For example, if I put this wafer down here and get a pen and press it hard in the centre, in theory I should get four separate pieces. That's because it's single crystal.

If you take a silicon wafer like this and put it out in sunlight, it'll just get hot. It won't actually, er, develop any electricity. We actually convert it into a photovoltaic generator by processing the solar cell through our production line. Basically the bigger the wafer, the more power that we get from the solar cell.

Language work

In the part of the sentence with *if*, Alistair uses the present tense. In the parts without *if* he uses *should* and *will*. He uses *will* when he is sure of what will happen, and *should* when he is not.

1 will become, heat;   2 don't process, won't produce;   3 test, shouldn't make;
4 should sell, believe;   5 will get, use;   6 develop, should save

2.2 The production process

Preview

1 C;   2 G;   3 F;   4 E;   5 D;   6 B;   7 A

First view

Step		Picture
1	clean the wafers	D
2	texturize the wafers	E
3	give the wafers photovoltaic ability	C
4	make the surfaces positive and negative	A
5	test the wafers	B

Second view

1 Step 3;   2 Step 3;   3 Step 4;   4 Step 2

ALISTAIR MITCHELL: The first stage in the process is to clean up the wafers.

The next stage in the process is called texturization. What we do is carry out a special surface treatment to the silicon. It puts tiny pyramids all the way across the silicon surface and what this does is to enhance the light absorption. The more light you get into a solar cell, the more power and current you get out.

The next step is to give it its photovoltaic ability. That's the ability to convert sunlight directly into electricity. The wafers are heated to around 1000 degrees C. Once the wafers are up to temperature, a special process gas is put into the tube. This converts one surface of the solar cell. The solar cell will now develop a voltage when exposed to sunlight.

The next step is to put on some conductive metal contacts. We do this by screen printing. We screen print aluminium and silver onto the back of the solar cell and pure silver onto the front of the solar cell. You have one surface which is positive and one surface which is negative.

The next thing that we do is test all of our solar cells. This ensures we get the maximum reliability in the modules and the maximum output power from our solar cells.

The solar panel is then connected to an external circuit, the current will flow and you can use that power to do whatever work you want: lighting, heating, do water pumping or whatever.

Language work

The verbs in the passive voice are: *is called*, *are heated*, *is put into*, *is then connected*.

Example answer

The first step is to clean the wafers. Then a special surface is created on the wafers to improve their ability to absorb light. This step is called texturization. The next step is to heat the wafer to 1000° C and to put a special gas into the tube. This gives the solar cell the ability to convert sunlight into electricity. Then conductive metal contacts are screen printed onto the surface, making one side positive and one negative. The solar cells are then tested. The last step is to connect them to an external circuit.

Further practice

1 light;   2 power;   3 current;   4 That's;   5 ability;   6 convert

Part 3 The market

Preview

1 kit;   2 infrastructure;   3 grid;   4 pump;   5 sector;   6 rural;   7 navigation

First, second and third views

1	business area	telecommunications	grid-connect	rural infrastructure	specialist
2	applications	telecommunications		water pumping systems lighting kits	navigation systems
3	regions		Europe USA Japan	Third World	Australia Europe Scandinavia sunbelt countries

Videoscript

KEN BROWN: We have put our business into what we classify as sectors. Telecommunications is one area.

Telecommunications is a developed market and, um, solar is a power source and when you're dealing with tops of mountain tops in very remote areas it is one of the only sources of energy that is economically viable.

The other area is, is grid-connect, and that is mainly driven into the European markets, um, interest in America and also Japan.

The other sector that we've got is what we classify as rural infrastructure and this is where we're now dealing usually into Third World type countries, supplying lighting kits, small power systems, um, water pumping systems, to areas where there is no, no infrastructure at all, very, very remote from the cities.

We also have another area in our business which we call specialist, and that particular area deals with, um, on the navigation side. A lot of the lights in harbours are all driven by solar power. Now that's not in countries just such as Australia, or the sunbelt countries, even in Europe and some of the Scandinavian countries.

Part 4 Four applications of the technology

4.1 The Peters ice cream trolley

Viewing task

1 specialist;   2 stay out (at work) longer;
3 No, it isn't. There are charged batteries as well.

Videoscript

RICHARD COLLINS: The ice cream trolley is an application that, would, really comes under the specialist sector. It doesn't drop into one of the traditional business sectors. But in their particular case they have a product that they wish to sell, they're away from the grid so they can't have a normal refrigerator. What they do is they charge the batteries up overnight from the mains – the product is cooled overnight as well – then they walk out with the trolleys, the vendor walks out with the trolleys into areas such as Darling Harbour or the Olympic site even. The batteries will discharge slowly over the day but having a solar module there ensures that the vendor can stay out all day and therefore maximizing time on the streets to be able to sell the product.

4.2 The Malaysian project

Preview

B

Viewing task

1 air;   2 sea;   3 road;   4 foot;   5 helicopters;   6 nine

Videoscript

KEN BROWN: It's shaping up as if there's going to be a major logistical problem as far as getting products into these remote areas. What have we really got in mind at this point in time? How are we going to approach this?

COLLEAGUE: We'll be using air transportation, sea transportation, and road, and if necessarily foot. In some cases, particularly the inland locations, particularly around the borders with Indonesia where the, the terrain is very mountainous and villages are very remote, we will be forced to use helicopters, and the overall project will take about nine months of installation.

Language work

1 really;   2 got;   3 in;   4 mind;   5 going;   6 approach

<u>What</u> have we <u>really</u> got in <u>mind</u> at this <u>point</u> in <u>time</u>?
<u>How</u> are we going to ap<u>proach</u> this?

The intonation is falling in both questions.
Most questions with *wh* question words or *how*, have a falling intonation.

4.3 The Homebush Bay project

Preview

1 C; 2 A; 3 D; 4 B

First view

1 In Sydney.
2 remote, environmentally friendly

Second view

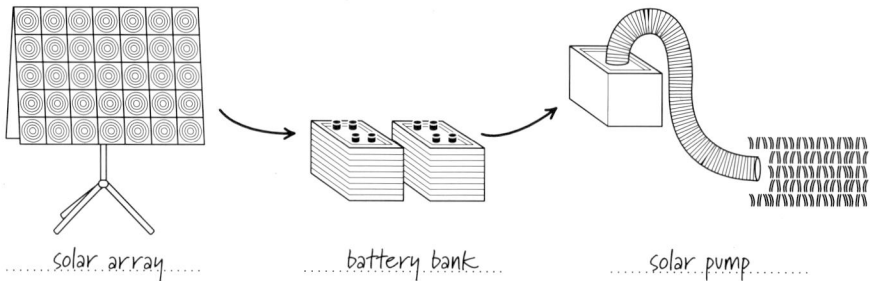

...... solar array .... battery bank .... solar pump ......

Videoscript

TONY STOCKEN: One of the particularly interesting urban solar applications we've got is a solar water pumping system.

This is Homebush Bay, the site of the 2000 Olympics in Sydney. We're actually standing on a remediated waste site. The solar pumping system is designed to pump excess nutrients from the remediated site to fertilize grassy areas.

The basic system, er, comprises a solar array, here, which then feeds to a battery bank which in turn powers a solar pump, which is located over here.

The client, the Waste Service in this case, required a pumping system which could work remote from the grid. Something that was environmentally friendly.

4.4 The Hawkesbury River House

Preview

1 mod cons; 2 back-up; 3 generator; 4 hybrid

First view

1 A basic system costs about *$10,000*.
2 A more sophisticated system costs about *$20,000*.
3 This is a *hybrid* system. The solar system is backed up by a *generator*.

Second view

1 Because there isn't any main supply of energy there.
2 Washing machine   Dryer   TV   Fridge   Hi-fi

Videoscript

TONY STOCKEN: The most basic system would be a solar power system to power your lights and that would probably start round about 1,000 dollars and going to your more sophisticated system powering all the, sort of, major appliances in your house and plus a few luxuries ... you're probably talking up to about 20,000 dollars.

HOME-OWNER: As there isn't any main supply of electricity here, we had to make a decision as to what sort of power we were going to have. And we looked at having just a generator and we realized that that wasn't going to be particularly efficient, given that we wanted to have all the mod cons in this house as we had in the city. So we explored that further and discovered that the best combination was to have what is called a hybrid system where you have solar and a generator, where the generator's a back-up to the solar system. Since we've been operating this system we have, certainly, become more aware that it is more environmentally friendly and very efficient. We have everything that you would find in a regular house in the city. So we have a washing machine, television, dryer, refrigerator, hi-fi system – everything like that.

Part 5 The future for solar energy

First view

1 consumer products
2 the developing countries
3 the developed countries

Second view

1 Solar power will be the ideal source for providing *social needs* to people in developing countries.
2 In developed countries, solar panels will become a *building* material.
3 When you build a house, the walls and roof will generate power, possibly feeding back into a *grid system* or *stored in batteries*.

Videoscript

KEN BROWN: Where do I see it going? Um, there'll be many different market places. I mean, you are going to see more consumer gidgets that use solar. Um, you'll see it used in the developing countries again because solar is an ideal type of power source for providing social needs to people in developing countries. In the developed countries, um, I believe ultimately and I'm not sure when this will be – in the next 10, 15, 20 years – it will become a building material. So when you build a house, the walls, the roof and that will become some form of active material which will then be generating power and possibly feeding back into a grid system or stored in batteries to be used within that household. I don't know when, when it's all going to happen but I'm very, very confident it will happen.

Language work

■ ▪ solar	■ ▪▪ silicon	▪ ■ enhance	▪■▪ develop	▪ ■ ▪▪ technology	▪ ▪■▪ application
current process circuit surface	energy property	ensure remote convert	efficient absorption	ability logistical	transportation

Follow-up

Example answer

As fossil fuels start to run out and global warming becomes a serious problem, solar technology will become much more sophisticated and more widely used. It will probably be manufactured throughout the world, not only in developed countries. More and more ways of using solar energy may be found. For example, solar panels could become a standard part of buildings. Solar power might also be used instead of petrol in engines, as petrol causes so many problems with pollution. However, solar cars will have to give people the same freedom they now enjoy with petrol-driven cars.

12

Thanks and acknowledgements

The authors and publishers would like to thank the following individuals and companies:

Roxanne Hudnall, Adrian Marrullier and Prince Sports Group; Chris Phippen, Caroline Poultney and Seafare; Andrea Berlowitz and Leapfrog Research and Planning; John Harford, Ken Brown and BP Solar; Peter Ravenscroft and Bruce Blake, cameramen; Peter Kyle, sound; Paul Pearson, VT editor; Andrew Lovett, music; Steve Kantor, voice-over.

The authors and publishers are grateful to the following companies who have given permission to reproduce copyright material and photographs:
pp 13 and 14 (left), BT Archives; p 14 (right), MOTOROLA Cellular Subscriber Division; pp 15 and 59, Prince Sports Group; pp 20 and 24, Seafare; p 40, Leapfrog Research and Planning; pp 43 and 74, BP; p 49, BP Solar.

Illustrations on pp 8, 9, 22, 28 and 52 by Kathy Baxendale; pp 7, 12, 20, 39 and 50 by Oxford Illustrators.
Design by Oxprint Design.